# FRENCH LITERARY IMAGINATION
## AND DOSTOEVSKY
## AND OTHER ESSAYS

# French Literary Imagination and Dostoevsky

## AND OTHER ESSAYS

## Henri Peyre

Studies in the Humanities No. 10
*Literature*

THE UNIVERSITY OF ALABAMA PRESS
*University, Alabama*

# CONTENTS

# FRENCH LITERARY IMAGINATION
## AND DOSTOEVSKY
## AND OTHER ESSAYS

# 1 French Literary Imagination and Dostoevsky

THE WISTFUL CONTEMPLATION of the misunderstandings that separate nations and of the distortions that the image of an artist undergoes when he is appraised outside his own country has always been one of the fascinating aspects of the comparative study of literatures. Several French scholars have specialized in the kaleidoscopic presentation of such mirages. There are writers among the greatest who appear to be ideal as catalysts, so sure is their touch in bringing out revealing chain reactions in those who, long after their deaths, submit to the impact of their works. Often they are at one and the same time the most national of authors and the most universal. They may, like Faulkner or Proust, have depicted nothing but a circumscribed geographical or social scene and, like Dostoevsky, have been intent on exploring the psychological and emotional depths of their own countrymen; the circle of their foreign admirers seems to be all the larger for it. Fortunately they have few imitators abroad, and that preserves the uniqueness of their work. They exercise small influence, especially if they happen to be too great to provoke in their successors that "anxiety of influence" which an anguished and brilliant critic, Harold Bloom, recently analyzed. But they elicit responses among the creative writers of another country that betray both the questions asked by those writers, unbeknownst to themselves, and aspects of their work perhaps unnoticed by their own countrymen.

At the forefront of such writers stands Dostoevsky. Surprisingly enough, the full history of his impact on several countries of Western Europe and of America appears to have tempted very few scholars in the last three or four decades. A volume entitled *Gide, Freedom and Dostoevsky* by Mischa H. Fayer, published in 1946 in Middlebury, Vermont, was too ambitious and not rigorous enough to have much validity today. The ablest study of the English reputation of the great Russian novelist, by Helen Muchnic, appeared in 1939; much has been written since in the country of D. H. Lawrence, Somerset Maugham, and Graham Greene concerning his fiction and his religious and political attitude. A number of theses must have been started, and perhaps completed, in American universities on Gide's relationship to Dostoevsky; none however occupies an eminent place among the many volumes devoted to Gide. The most conscientious survey of the French critics of Dostoevsky is by a German scholar, Hans Friedrich Minssen. His dissertation on *Die französische Kritik und Dostoevsky* was presented at Hamburg as early as 1933, long before Mauriac, Claudel, the existentialists, and Camus had expressed themselves on the Russian giant.

A French specialist of Russian may someday scrutinize the translations of Dostoevsky's fiction done in France since the early, and avowedly unfaithful, version of *The Brothers Karamazov* by Halpérine-Kaminski. Several scholars will be needed to survey the reviews and the articles concerning those French translations and the volumes on Dostoevsky published since World War I; 1914 was the date at which F. W. J. Hemmings closed his excellent study of *The Russian Novel in France, 1884–1914* (Oxford Univ. Press, 1950). The impact of the Russian-born thinkers and writers who had emigrated from Russia to France and who interpreted Dostoevsky to the French has not yet been weighed. It would form a revealing chapter of a history of the Russian intellectual migration that followed 1917; the names of Berdiaev, Levinson, Pozner, Troyat stand out among many other interpreters of Dostoevsky in French. All that may be attempted in this essay is an analysis of the portrayals of Dostoevsky and of the most striking personal statements on his world by a few imaginative writers of France. The selection made is arbitrary, and exhaustiveness is obviously not the goal.

The French usually have not been considered the readiest nation to acclaim and to translate authors from foreign countries. When they have done so, however, it has often been with an enthusiasm that quickly proved contagious. They transfigured Walter Scott and Byron, Schiller and Goethe, later D'Annunzio and Faulkner. But they passed on their own vision of those authors to other lands. Professor Hemmings called the sudden vogue of Russian fiction in France in the 1880's an invasion, which he playfully compared to that of the Cossacks who had frightened the Parisians in 1814. He generously credited Eugène Melchior de Vogüé, a predecesor of Vogüé named Courrière (in 1875), and an original critic who died young, Émile Hennequin (in 1889), with the earliest, and for many years the very best, appreciations of Dostoevsky in Western Europe. Indeed, the novelist's own compatriots had in large numbers remained cool, or outright hostile, to a novelist in whom, like many Soviet critics later, during the Zhdanovian era, they refused to see a faithful portrayer of Russia.[1] The biographers of Dostoevsky have often quoted the revulsion of a typical one among those enlightened Russians, Count Kutchelev-Bezborodko, who, reading one of the early novels, *The Insulted and the Injured,* exclaimed that the author could not possibly be depicting Russians; the behavior of such outlandish characters would be admissible, and perhaps true to life, in France or in Belgium, but certainly not in Russia.[2]

The tide of translations and of laudatory comments that Vogüé had unleashed in 1886 subsided by the end of the century. None of the novelists who may be said to have been influenced by Dostoevsky (the Swiss Édouard Rod and the French Charles Louis Philippe being the most prominent) had power enough to assimilate the lessons that they read in their bewildering and overpowering model. The general trend in France, in the first decade of the twentieth century, ran in reaction against foreign literary imports and against the eccentricities, as they were then taken to be, of symbolism. It fell to a prosewriter who soon was to found a literary chapel and to take over the leadership of the young, André Gide, to launch a revival of enthusiasm for Dostoevsky in France. He had almost reached the age of forty and was putting the finishing touches to his first truly influential novel, *La Porte étroite* (1909), when, in 1908, he published his first article on Dostoevsky. In 1910, Jacques Co-

4

peau, then thirty-one, boldly but not very successfuly dramatized and performed *The Brothers Karamazov* at the Théâtre des Arts. Claudel, Suarès, Proust, Faure, the four important writers who expressed themselves with passion and insight on Dostoevsky, were, like Gide, born around 1870.

Gide's volume first appeared in English translation in 1925, with an introduction by Arnold Bennett, today neglected as a novelist, but far from insignificant as an open-minded critic of literature. It has since been reprinted many times, and Albert L. Guérard wrote a sensitive and discriminating preface to the edition of the volume published by New Directions in 1961. It is made up of a 1908 lecture on Dostoevsky as seen in his letters, of six more lectures delivered in 1922 at the theater of the Vieux Colombier in Paris, and of another short address on *The Brothers Karamazov*. The tone is casual and almost conversational. The lecturer quotes extensively from the novels, from the letters, and from the journalistic articles of Dostoevsky. Nowhere does he treat any of the novels systematically or analyze them from the point of view of their fictional technique. A few aspects of the novelist's personality are stressed repeatedly. Others are neglected. Gide never attempted to be a systematic critic of other writers, be they Stendhal, Goethe, Nietzsche, Montaigne, Baudelaire, or others most dear to him at some time or other. His remarks are all the more percipient for being the desultory, but very penetrating, notes of an amateur who writes with the closeness of approach that often accrues from love. The book is avowedly a self-portrait, and Gide made no bones about it. He deliberately went to what, in Dostoevsky, had struck him; and what struck him, in 1908-18, while he was going through a long personal crisis and experienced the necessity for a reorientation of his whole career, was what he then needed most. In that sense, that volume, the only full volume written by Gide on another author, elaborated on from his fortieth to his fifty-third year, is indeed the crucial book, "le livre-charnière," of his long career.

Steeping himself in the Dostoevskian ocean in those years led Gide to reflect on the technique of fiction more steadily than he had done when composing his earlier, and personal, novels, *L'Immoraliste* and *La Porte étroite*. *Les Faux-Monnayeurs* and the diary he kept while composing that novel, his first genuine one, as he was to proclaim, as well as the epistolary and conversational exchanges with Martin Du Gard bear the traces of that intensive Gidian reflection. But there is relatively little on the craft of fiction in the lectures. Gide probably realized that Dostoevsky's vision conditioned his art, that a Frenchman might conceivably borrow something from Turgenev's narrative art, perhaps even a certain tone and a smooth rendering of the emotional ordeals of the characters from Tolstoy, but that few lessons profitably could be learned from the structure of *The Demons* (as *The Possessed* is designated here) or from the impassioned discussions between the sons of old Karamazov. Gide, who had admired Stendhal in his youth, shared with him a certain shyness about believing wholeheartedly in his characters and about wrenching credibility from the reader. Like Stendhal, he refused to indulge in the physical description of his heroes; he multiplied personal interventions and side remarks, apologizing for the behavior of his characters or judging them with playful irony. More than once, he argued that the art of design was the privilege of the French, as contrasted with the Germans in particular. He praised Racine and La Bruyère, *Les Liaisons dangereuses* and even *Dominique* as embodying what is most satisfying in that art—a sensuousness of the intellect, a frail delicacy of line, an avoidance of overstatement. Dostoevsky showed him how much power could lie in the very opposite of that French tradition. He became intoxicated with that headier wine; he rolled in that turmoil in which the linear succession of events, the discreet analysis of moods were drowned. But he had the wisdom not to attempt to assume a personality that was not his or to ape a genius that he worshipped as alien to him. Eventually, with *L'Ecole des femmes, Geneviève, Thésée,* Gide was to return to an even thinner substance and to an even sketchier neatness of outline than he had evinced in his more disturbed and inwardly vibrating novels. Throughout his period of enthusiasm for Communist Russia and during his travels in that country and in the *Journals* he kept in his latter years, he seldom mentioned the vision of Russia that he had owed to Dostoevsky. He could devour and then discard his successive literary loves with the supreme egoism of a Goethe.

The tone of Gide's lectures is that of a neophyte, well aware that nothing valid can be achieved without enthusiasm and that the privilege of enthusiasm is to prove communicative before it flags. His rather sudden conversion to Dostoevsky carried with it some pride at his being among the first Frenchmen wholeheartedly to espouse everything in those "loose baggy monsters," as Henry James had called the Russian novelists before whom he stood, frightened. He delighted in his lectures in aiming a few barbs at the timid taste of the French aristocrat and academician who had first introduced Dostoevsky to a wide public, Count de Vogüé. He also relished opposing his new idol to what he considered the French tradition of storytelling, that of Lesage, Voltaire, Stendhal, in which the whole of the picture receives an equal light and glaring effects are avoided. Such, in truth, might also be said to have been the Russian tradition with Gogol, Leskov, Tolstoy, and others. In contrast with that equally diffused light or that panoramic vision, as Percy Lubbock calls it, stand Dostoevsky's lurid effects, with a glaring light illuminating one feature or one happening, the rest remaining steeped in darkness as in a Rembrandt painting. Such effects were not unknown to Balzac. But Gide's exaltation of Dostoevsky made him unfair to many effects in Balzac's fiction that had been enormously admired by the Russian author; Dostoevsky had, after all, translated *Eugénie Grandet* and drawn some inspiration from George Sand's *Mauprat* in *Poor Folk* and even in *The Brothers Karamazov*. Rightly, Gide asserted that the turmoil in Dostoevsky's turbid characters and their sudden inconsistencies could not hide the masterful organization of those complex, meandering novels. The opening scenes in *The Idiot*, for example, and the subtle conjuring up of the right atmosphere at the beginning of *The Eternal Husband* are no less admirable in their artistry, if less mathematically calculated, than the beginnings of *Madame Bovary* or of *L'Education sentimentale*. Still, Gide's main interest lay elsewhere. Even in *Les Faux-Monnayeurs,* the only work in which he attempted to weave the threads of four or five different plots into a multicolored skein, he kept shy of those scenes of confrontation between several protagonists; he likewise avoided those passionate metaphysical and moral debates that, in the Russian novelist, are made to be part and parcel of the action. He favored instead the typically Gidian device of the private diary, in which relentlessly introspective characters, Alissa or Edouard, the would-be novelist, jot down their intentions and their frustrations, shunning all the while any dramatic confrontation with the others who would deprive them of their secret charm.

Gide's typical novel is a novel of ideas in the sense that the Protestant pastor, whom he acknowledged to lurk in him behind the mischievous and boyish ironist, cannot long resist drawing lessons from events. But he realized early in his career the perils inherent in the "novel of ideas" for a compatriot of Paul Bourget, who had portentously specialized in that type of fiction and theorized on it in his preface to *La Terre promise*. A novelist of ideas probably should not be too clear a thinker. Else, having started with a body of lucid conclusions reached before he invents his characters, he would be tempted to assume a superior attitude and to turn his creatures into mouthpieces for his views. It is best for him to start from a chaos of impulses and anguished reflections, which will tear the characters asunder until they effect their own resolution of their inner conflicts. He thinks his story in terms of scenes, not in terms of characters.

At the very time when he was reflecting on Dostoevsky, Gide was introduced tò the novels of George Meredith and of Henry James. He had, for a time, enjoyed the intellectual games of the former and encouraged the publication by the firm of Gallimard of a translation of the allegorical *Shaving of Shagpat*. He soon wearied of it. Charles du Bos, of whom he saw a great deal in those years, endeavored to make Gide a devotee of Henry James. As was often the case with Gide, he found his own truth and formulated it most forcefully through asserting his differences from a friend. In the fall of 1920, he sent Charles du Bos a thoughtful and firm letter, which he deemed significant enough to publish it in the tenth volume of his *Oeuvres complètes* (pp. 547-50). In it, he condemned Henry James in the name of a Dostoevskian aesthetics. The American, he submitted, might be important for Britain. But he was not for the French, for whom an excess of intellectuallity in their imaginative works was the permanent danger. One senses with James that he controls his narrative too surely; he does not involve himself in it. Restraint, economy of means, consistent pursuit of a single point of view—he has all that and thereby appeals to the reader's intellect. But he captures only the intellect of his characters also, and one deplores in them the lack of flesh, the absence of wild and dark forces unleashed. They only live in, and through, their relations among themselves, hence on a social and horizontal plane. "Nothing divine inhabits them." They are not the abodes, or the victims, of blind forces suddenly irrupting into them. They are, in other words, too remote from Dostoevskian characters, "created, like Eve, out of the very flesh of their maker" and tortured by the novelist's own anguish.

The same claim is made throughout the volume on Dostoevsky. When the Russian novelist thinks in his own name, as in the *Journal of an Author,* he declaims, utters prophecies (seldom to be fulfilled) on political and social matters in an awkward style. He then can rave as wildly as Balzac does in his discourses of a doctor of social sciences. Abstract thinking does not serve a novelist to advantage, if he attempts to incorporate that thinking into his fiction; others besides Balzac and Dostoevsky have found that out at their own expense, from Tolstoy to D. H. Lawrence. But when ideas are lived "as functions of the characters" and when "the cross fertilizing of fact and idea" has taken place, a living profundity is reached that makes the debates in *The Demons* or the parables in *The Brothers Karamazov* far more haunting than any abstract and bodyless treatment of ideas. Gide had wrestled with the Christian temptation, apparently for the last time in his life, during the years of World War I and of crisis in his relations with his wife. He then watched several of his friends convert to Catholicism, wondered in *Numquid et tu?* whether he was not destined, he too, to avow himself "a Galilean," then dismissed the lure of the refuge of faith with *La Symphonie pastorale* in 1919.

He nevertheless continued to nurture secretly the conviction that his originality lay in his having lived his Christian faith for many years, in having known Christ's message first-hand through the Gospels, and in remaining true to that message even while repudiating the interpretations of it offered by the several churches. At the outset, in his lectures on Dostoevsky, he defined the fundamental originality of the Russian over all other novelists as the exploration of a new type of relationship: not between man and woman, nor between man and other men; not the conflicts of passion and intellect, of the individual with his family or with society; but the relations between the self and God. Dostoevsky had been arrogantly convinced that the Russians were the only Christian people. To Gide, he was the only truly Christian novelist. Irked as he often was by friends and critics who, taking advantage of Gide's generosity in proclaiming his admiration for other writers, ascribed to them an over-magnified influence on him, Gide liked to retort that he had been, on his own, groping or rushing toward Dostoevsky (as he had previously done toward Nietzsche) long before he actually encountered him. He was then laying bare his need and his call for him. He made the point most forcefully in a curious letter of March 2, 1918, to his Belgian friend André Ruyters, published in the *Australian Journal of French Studies* (7, Nos. 1–2, 1970, pp. 17–22). He had just reread *The Idiot,* after receiving a question from his friend, and he seized the opportunity to proclaim Dostoevsky's "deep influence" over him. But he added that his own evolution had already prepared him for that encounter with the Russian novelist, "whose influence merged with that of the Gospel." He contended that Ruyters' lack of knowledge of the Gospel (somewhat self-righteously Gide deplored that lack of familiarity with the Gospels in most of his Catholic friends) stood in the way of his understanding Dostoevsky. He went on:

> He is, I believe, the *only* Christian author I know (or, if you prefer, whom I acknowledge as such. Others are Catholic, or Protestant, *before* they are Christian. For the Gospel often stands in opposition to the Churches. As soon as I discovered Dostoevsky (but I believe I already knew him in part), I steeped myself into his works and told myself: At last! That one did understand!

In his lectures, Gide dismissed not only Stendhal, Flaubert, Zola, who like Proust later had indeed lived outside Christianity, but also Balzac, a Catholic of a sort. Granting little attention to Balzac's Swedenborgian novel and to his mysticism, Gide contended, not unrightly, that only in Dostoevsky were man's relations with

God explored and placed at the very root of the characters' thoughts, feelings, and acts. Through *The Idiot* in particular, Gide insisted that he received "a true illumination" that brought home to him the full significance of Christ's admonition: "Whosoever shall not receive the Kingdom of God as a little child, he shall not enter therein" (Mark 10.15). He undestood, as he read of the strange state of almost supernatural well-being experienced by Prince Muishkin just before his epileptic fit, the bliss of suddenly feeling like a small child.

It is, however, another one of Christ's sayings, which he usually quoted according to Luke (17.33), that was brought obsessively to Gide's mind by his meditation on Dostoevsky: "Whosoever shall seek to save his life shall lose it; and whosoever shall lose his life shall preserve it." That became to Gide the main religious, ethical, and even aesthetic lesson that he drew from the novelist, as well as the sharpest point of contrast between him and so-called "western" psychology. From Corneille to Balzac, French literature (and Spanish or English, stressing the code of honor and the ideal of the gentleman, differed even more from Russian) appeared to Gide to be oriented toward the assertion of the will. The characters aspire to be heroes and, accordingly, to become the ones they want to be; they strain every nerve to mold themselvs according to an ideal that has been instilled in them through education and culture. If they become aware of contradictions in themselves, they endeavor to reconcile them, or else they ignore them.[3] They may suffer humiliation at the hands of others, but they seldom experience humility. Their pride (as gentlemen, as would-be stoics, as husbands) is the last thing they would renounce. Their intellect bows to charity only with immense difficulty, even if they are called Pascal or Bossuet. The same sense of self-respect forbids them to admit blatant inconsistencies in themselves. They desperately want to believe in a certain unity of man, and they refuse to harbor, at the same moment, contradictory impulses.

Not so with Raskolnikov in his behavior toward Sonia or with the strange protagonist of *The Eternal Husband*. Gide realized how primary in Dostoevsky's psychological makeup is the obsession of a "ménage à trois," another form of the "Double" that the novelist had conjured up in one of his shorter novels. The husband positively needs the other man, his wife's lover or his fiancée's ravisher, in order to justify, or even to experience, his own love. Jealousy, Gide hints, an artificial and conventional feeling with many of us Westerners, is absent from Dostoevsky's characters and is at no time needed to prolong desire or to cause a dead love to revive from its ashes. Indeed, the less physical the love is, the stronger it proves for those characters. To them, paragons of genuine Christianity, the sole triumph lies in the renouncing of their individuality.

It is not difficult to surmise that the divorce between physical and spiritual love, the nonfulfillment of love in many Dostoevskian characters held especial appeal to the Frenchman who had experienced in his own "amazing marriage," and justified to himself, a similar divorce between respect for the person loved spiritually and the urges of the flesh. Even the theme of the "ménage à trois" was more readily congenial to Gide than to other Westerners, since he well knew that he, like Michel in L'Immoraliste, had in a sense needed his wife to be a witness (the word in Greek was "a martyr") to his own flirtations with boys or adolescents. The urge to confess publicly that which society must consider as most dishonorable, which is present in Raskolnikov and apparently was also in Dostoevsky, has surprised many an observer of Russia since Custine first described it as a deeply seated feature of the "Russian soul." It found in Gide a sympathetic observer. He himself had not resisted, in Saul, in his early novels, then in his own autobiography, and in Corydon, a similar urge to cry aloud what most of his friends, through prudence or cowardice, were advising him to conceal. He would again, after the peak of his enthusiasm for Dostoevsky, throw conventional wisdom to the winds and delight in proclaiming in lyrical outbursts, with no fear of ridicule, his admiration for communism. He was to assert then that not Marx, but the Gospel (which he had read more assiduously than he ever did Marx) had brought him to his new, and short-lived, faith. Throughout, he perceived a harmony between Dostoevskian characters and precepts and the verses of the Gospel, which he interpreted in a highly personal way: the one in particular, more typical in the French Bible since the French word "scandale" has very different connotations from its English counterpart and from the English rendering as "offences" in the English Bible, in which Matthew has Christ exclaim: "Woe unto the world because of offenses ("les scandales") for it must needs that scandals come" (Matt. 18.7).

Two other motives, or obsessions, in Dostoevsky's fiction fascinated Gide for a time. Again, they answered concerns that had long been his, and Gide found in them a confirmation of what he carried within himself but had been too timid as yet to voice. One is the famous "gratuitous act," which a character in *The Demons* had hailed as altogether unmotivated, hence free, and brandished as a challenge to God by a man absolutely undetermined in his decisions and choosing suicide. Gide made less metaphysical use of the theme, and of the phrase, but for a time he read into those inexplicable deeds (more often misdeeds, or crimes such as the one that Lafcadio commits during a train ride) revelations on the complexities of human nature.

Of the other, the existence of the Devil as an active force in us, Gide made less felicitous use in his fiction. The scene in which the Evil One visits Olivier in *Les Faux-Monnayeurs* is probably the least convincing in the novel. One senses at times that the Frenchman felt he *had* to believe in the objective existence of "the Adversary" because Dostoevsky had made it credible, somewhat as a young Frenchman traveling in Scotland feels he *must* believe in ghosts, because he has read ghost stories located in Scotland. The fifth lecture in the Dostoevsky volume makes much of the Manichean character of his religion and of the fact that the Evil One resides, not in what is commonly viewed as the basest or the most carnal in us, but in the very seat of the intellect and of our reason. It thus happened that, in the years when he pored over *The Demons* most rapturously, Gide was just discovering two English poets whom, rather arbitrarily, he saw as parallel, or as close, to the Russian: Robert Browning, who stands at the opposite pole from Dostoevsky, if anywhere, and William Blake, from whom Gide only picked a few sayings out of context. The relationship he sets up among the three authors, to whom he adds a fourth one, Nietzsche, is fortuitous and purely artificial, as his brother-in-law, writing under the pseudonym of Michel Arnauld, was prompt to remark in reviewing

Gide's *Dostoevsky* in the *Nouvelle Revue française* of July 1923. Neither could Nietzsche pass for an advocate of humility nor might Browning be caricatured into a pessimist haunted by man's degradation. Gide must, soon after, have admitted it to himself, because he became fond of quoting the Victorian poet as a believer in the splendid future awaiting man if he would grow instead of stopping, and he contemplated rosy vistas for mankind if it adopted an idealized form of communism.[4]

It would be idle, and too facile, to take issue with several aspects of the hidden presentation of Dostoevsky. It has already been said, and Gide confessed it, that the volume of personal criticism has many features of a self-portrait. Carried away by his eagerness to convert his audience, the speaker also was endeavoring to convince himself as he spoke and wrote. Annoyed as he had been by some of his embarrassingly self-righteous Catholic friends and by their self-assurance after their conversion (Francis Jammes, Claudel, Ghéon, du Bos), he delighted in emphasizing Dostoevsky's anti-Catholicism and in opposing Catholicism to genuine Christianity. He likewise revealed an inadequate knowledge of Balzac when he characterized Balzac's fiction, at the end of his second lecture, as "having sprung from the contact between the Gospels and the Latin mind," while Dostoevsky's had grown from the "contact between the Gospels and Buddhism." Gide even rashly equated Buddhism with that strange entity "the Asiatic mind," presumably covering Japanese Taoism, Chinese Confucianism as well as Iran and India. There occurs more than one non sequitur in Gide's analysis of the characters in Dostoevsky, in whom the simultaneous coexistence of totally opposite personalities is said (at the end of the fourth lecture) to stem from renunciation of the self; that, for Gide, was the enriching sacrifice by him who immolates his own ego and thereby "saves his life for Christ's sake." The evangelical saying came to imply, for Gide, that *that* writer turns out to be the most powerful who loses himself in every one of his works and who becomes every one of his characters.

To a large extent, Gide's Dostoevskian crusade was one of the aspects of his struggle, between 1910 and 1925 (and especially during the nationalistic rage that seized France and other European countries during World War I), against the narrow complacency of his countrymen, too fond of relying on their French tradition. Hence some animadversion against La Rochefoucauld, Corneille, Balzac, who were viewed as failing to make an allowance for the contradictions in man and for the coexistence of conflicting, and equally authentic, sentiments. Hence also a rather naive conviction that jealousy is an artificial reaction in the Western lover or husband, resting on an egoistical and false conception of outraged honor, and that Russian males are immune from it. So was J. J. Rousseau, so indeed were many husbands in eighteenth-century libertine novels (and in life), and not a few in Balzacian fiction. The Russians who have read Gide's volume, if several oral conversations with them may be judged to be representative, have declared the generalizations on the Russian psyche most arbitrary and the general picture of their novelist as typically that of a foreigner who insists upon seeing the Russians as incurably exotic, non-Western, Asiatic, or Oriental. Some of them prefer to consider themselves as the truest inheritors of ancient Greece and, in their music, their painting, their poets, and their storytellers, as the champions of the truest classical values. A random remark of T. E. Lawrence in one of his letters (No. 281, Jan. 15, 1926) would probably be endorsed by most Russian readers of Gide's volume, and by a number of non-Russians as well: "Gide's book on Dostoevsky was not good. He tried to make him into a Protestant and didn't get to grips with his real powers and depths. Few Frenchmen could. They are too dapper to feel as untidily and recklessly as the Russians."

Gide was not unaware of some artificiality in his delineation of Dostoevsky's religious and philosophical attitudes. He had depicted his own need for the kind of message that he read into the Russian novelist, or that he lent to him, forsaking temporarily the strictures that might have been formulated against some of the excesses in the characterization or in the ideological outpourings of Dostoevsky. In January 1922, he had jotted down in his *Journals* a note telling of the difficulty that he was experiencing in composing those lectures, in which he felt emotionally involved: "It will be, at least as much as a work of criticism, a volume of confessions . . . or rather, a profession of faith." In the third lecture, he had, with fairness and slight embarrassment, quoted a few lines that a young friend of his, whom he had entrusted with the direction of the *Nouvelle Revue française,* Jacques Rivière, had published in that periodical in February 1922. That brief article, mentioned by René Wellek in his introduction to the collection of critical essays on Dostoevsky that he edited for Twentieth Century Views, is one of the most lucid statements on the Russian novelist by a critic voicing, in very measured terms, the reservations that a cool-headed Frenchman might offer to the glorification of the great Slav.

Rivière nourished none of the nationalist prejudices that, in the years following World War I, were inciting a number of French traditionalists to rise in an indignant "defence of the West" and to crusade against the corrupting Russian influence. He had, early, been an enthusiast of Russian music and, as a prisoner of war in Germany in 1914–17, he had felt drawn to the charity and the fraternity shown by his Russian fellow-prisoners. Nor was he a narrow partisan of the French classics, even when he reiterated his attachment to the virtues of analytical lucidity and of neat design, which he praised in those whom he once called "his masters, those who refuse darkness, Descartes, Racine, Marivaux, Ingres" (*Nouvelle Revue française,* April 1925, p. 398). He had gone through successive raptures of enthusiasm for Claudel, then for Gide, and then, after the war, for Proust and for Freud. Gidian, he was profoundly, in the sense that he would collect himself after having wholly surrendered to a writer whom he had inordinately admired; he would promptly offset the influence of one master by submitting to a very different one.

After 1919, as the war-weary French were attempting to get back their moorings amid the wreckage of Europe and to speculate on the directions in which literature might go, Rivière expressed the hope that unbridled emotionalism and the wordy cult of intuition would not rule men of letters, who were faced with the necessity of proposing new values. In an article that appeared simultaneously in German and in French in November 1921, he derided some hyperbolical statements by one of his elders, André Suarès, in an essay on Dostoevsky.[5] "The creative emotion is the only true knowledge. . . . All ideas must merge into love." The rational and critical intellect was declared by Suarès to be a mere impediment. Rivière never sided with the fanatics of rationalism. He well knew, having tried his hand at the analytical novel himself, that the critical spirit, left to itself, is barren. Still, he insisted upon maintaining a balance between the two traditions and not excluding either of the two different atitudes open to a creator.

The novelist, Rivière argued with perhaps excessive neatness in his classification, in the process of creating and of presenting a character, can either stress his complexity or underline his coherence. He may reproduce all that is dark, abysmal in the character and plunge us also into that abyss, or he may explore those contradictions. Gide, in his lectures, was praising the cohabitation, within the same being, of contradictory instincts and of unreconciled, and unreconcilable, emotions. Dostoevsky appeared to him as perhaps the first writer to have "embraced that absurdity as an ideal." He also tended, Rivière insinuated, to exaggerate the disorder in his characters, and he then delighted in gaping at those contradictory beings as altogether unfathomable. He abstained from attempting to organize or to order those turbid Slavic souls.

Not so with the French, whom Rivière peremptorily reduced to one typical attitude. Their very description of a complex character is already an attempt of some sort at organizing it, at integrating his contrary moods and impulses. They must discover, or invent, the inner link behind those fighting elements. They try to leave no gap, no interstice, through which the unknown might surge up. They are afraid of "the vertigo of the human soul." Is the Russian way necessarily superior?

Rivière readily proclaimed how much he owed to the discovery of Dostoevsky and how puny at first the French novelists had appeared to him when he compared them to that uncouth, formidable colossus. And yet? Cannot that depth stem from an illusion? Are depths really meaningful, and worthwhile, if we do not descend into them? Are the people who behave in an unaccountable fashion necessarily deeper, more complex, truer than the others? Cannot a novelist endow a character both with depth and with coherence? In cogent terms, Rivière continued:

... In the end, the human being ... never escapes a certain deep-rooted logic. ... Even when he contradicts himself, is that contradiction anything else than the refraction of a single tendency? ... In psychology, the true depth is that which is explored.

There might conceivably arise a novelist who would go further even than Dostoevsky, by taking into account the contradictions and abysses of human nature and still seeking the link, or the hidden law, underlying those baffling inconsistencies. Neither Balzac nor Zola was a rationalist; yet their characters do act unreasonably, and also against reason, at times, but they still obey a certain inner law. The coexistence of contradictions may be, after all, a superficial affair and serve as an excuse for the novelist who is reluctant to look any deeper. Gide refrained from coming to terms with the objection formulated by Rivière, which he was content simply to quote.

The writer whom young Rivière had worshipped as the embodiment of sheer genius and as the one whose indomitable religious faith might perhaps bestow some unity upon his own versatile and overcritical nature was Paul Claudel. Claudel and Gide had known each other for many years, but had seen little of each other, when Gide published his *Dostoevsky.* Their friendship had cooled markedly after Claudel had realized that he would never succeed in converting his elusive friend to Catholic orthodoxy, or to so-called sexual orthodoxy. Still, when, from his post at the French embassy in Tokyo, Claudel received Gide's *Dostoevsky,* he congratulated him with warmth. He had himself long admired the Russian novelist, ranking him as high as his other unreserved admirations—Euripides, Virgil, Beethoven. Even the novelist's severity toward the Catholic Church, against which his prejudices had never relented, found grace in the eyes of Claudel. Claudel had more than once, and perversely, uttered foolish, dogmatic, and grossly unjust statements and could forgive the prophecies and the bland assertions of the author of *The Demons.* When Dostoevsky spoke in his own name, and not as a novelist, he could be discounted. However, behind that intemperance, Claudel noted in his interesting letter of thanks to Gide (July 29, 1923) that there always lay a strange reserve, "something essential which Dostoevsky obstinately kept silent and which tortured him to the end."

At the same time, and rightly, he offered the regret that the artist in Dostoevsky, with his splendid gift for composition, similar to Beethoven's, had been inadequately treated in Gide's lectures. Much later, in the conversations that the aged Claudel held with Jean Amrouche and which were published in 1954 as *Mémoires improvisés,* Claudel returned to the point, lauding the composition in Dostoevsky's fiction, and more particularly the symphonic opening of *The Idiot. The Brothers Karamazov,* he added in answer to a question from his interviewer, although unfinished and being a juxtaposition of fragments, is an even more majestic achievement. And the dramatist revealed that, in "a purely formal sense," he had learned much from that novel:

> From that point of view, I learned much from Dostoevsky, just as I would say that I learned much from Beethoven, whom I deciphered at that time with one finger. I found much analogy between their systems of composition. They are very copious, they forget nothing. To us, French, it may look like an excess of abundance, but all the same there is there a most remarkable art and unity of purpose.

In the same conversation, Claudel acclaimed the Russian novelist as one of the chief builders of his spirit: "The beginnings of my dramatic technique and of my vision of the world are to be found in that encounter with Dostoevsky." He hailed him as the inventor of polymorphous character, in opposition to the French classics, who portray characters all of a piece. The characters of the Russian novelist undergo sudden spontaneous mutations, as may be undergone by plants, according to the views of the biologist De Vries, who had impressed Claudel. Dostoevsky's discovery was to show man as a creature unknown to himself, encompassing within himself the strangest possibilities. From that view of character, the Christian poet and dramatist had learned, he acknowledged, "not to despair, always to be in a state of availability." To no other writer, not even to Shakespeare or to Balzac, not even to the Old Testament Prophets whom he commented upon unweariedly at the end of his life, has Claudel paid such a warm tribute.

While he was still in his twenties, Claudel met, at the home of Maurice Pottecher, a mutual friend, a strange, ardent, aloof Frenchman, born like him in 1868 and like him fiercely independent, so independent that, after leaving the Ecole Normale Supérieure, he had spurned any academic career and rejected all means of livelihood. His name was André Suarès. Claudel subsequently had an exchange of letters with him that is perhaps the most revealing of any of his volumes of correspondence. He thought for a time that he might succeed in converting Suarès, of Jewish origin and an agnostic, to Catholicism. He failed in the end, but no ill will resulted from Suarès' dallying with the thought of embracing Claudel's religion, as it did with Gide. Claudel, in the process and in order to break Suarès' umbrageous isolation, had persuaded him to meet André Gide. In December 1908, both men were pleased to make each other's acquaintance and to wonder at their mutual brilliance.

Soon, however, they asserted their differences. Suarès found Gide too Protestant, too critical, too elusive also, and a little superficial. Gide resented some of the hyperbolic praise that Suarès heaped upon men whom he found unworthy of such admiration, like D'Annunzio and Brunetière. In 1910 the rift between them deepened. Gide was then contemplating writing on Dostoevsky, and he suspected that Suarès was stealing the idea from him; Suarès had indeed offered to Péguy a *Cashiers de la Quinzaine* that would be devoted to the Russian novelist.[6] Suarès' long, rapturous essay appeared in fact in *La Grande Revue* (February 25, 1911, pp. 729–38; March 25 and April 10, 1911, pp. 225–46 and 555–76). It then became part of a volume, *Trois Hommes: Pascal, Ibsen, Dostoevsky,* which was eventually taken over by the editions of the *Nouvelle Revue française* (1919). Jacques Copeau, Gide's and Claudel's friend, reviewed Suarès' *Dostoevsky* at length and with warmth in *La Nouvelle Revue française* of February 1912 (pp. 226–41). Again in 1926, in a volume entitled *Présences,* Suarès included a review of a Dostoevsky commemoration at Copeau's theater, which had taken place on December 24, 1921. Next to Vogüé and Gide, Suarès is the French man of letters who, outside the academic community and long before any specialists of Slavic studies devoted their attention to the Russian writer, did most to rally his countrymen to Dostoevsky.

Suarès never was a cool and detached critic. He had either to hate or to love. His tone was consistently dramatic, even apocalyptic. He could be nothing if not fervently passionate. Even more than Gide, he wrote in lofty, rapturous strains, on Dostoevsky and on himself. At the outset, he cried out: "In him, I want to discern myself." And, like his model, Suarès wished to be loved. Like him he suffered from lack of recognition and from dismal poverty. He echoed several of the most pathetic outbursts of the Russian novelist in his letters of a perpetual beggar: "How can I write, while I am starving?" He retold the story of his pitiful life in vivid and lurid detail. He even espoused the novelist's claim that the Russians are "the God-bearing people" and would ultimately save Europe: "It is with Dostoevsky that, at last, Russia ceases to be Cossack and looms as a reserve for the future, as a resource for mankind."

Stendhal himself, whom Suarès admired and later followed in his Italian journeys, is immolated by him to Dostoevsky, in exalted and none too accurate terms: "What Stendhal is to pure intellect and to the mechanics of the automaton, Dostoevsky is to order and to the fatality of sentiments. . . . Dostoevsky is the prodigy of sentimental analysis and the greatest innovator known in that realm. . . . His art is a direct picture of intuition. That is why everything, with him, being profoundly true, resembles dream."

Suarès never was very "Cartesian" himself, nor did he ever compose a volume with rigor or patience. He wallowed with delight in what he termed Dostoevsky's occasional "prodigious disorder." But when he does have order, that order is no less prodigious. In him, as in Shakespeare, as in Rembrandt, "everything is attuned to the rhythm of love. Intelligence is the plough, not the seed or the harvest." He proves especially successful as the creator of tragic clowns, of those buffoons who "love themselves unreservedly, like monsters or children; and who love life, as if they were saints." Suarès was among the first in France to admire, as Camus would do much later, those enormous and tortured comic personages of the novelist—Lebedev, Marmeladov, old Karamazov. And he was the first also to praise Dostoevsky's delineation of women, a stumbling block in his novels for most Frenchmen:

> He feels a burning and sorrowful tenderness for women. He seems to need to suffer through them; he hates to make them suffer, and yet he realizes that he will always be for them an occasion for suffering. . . . He seeks the virgin in every woman; she is the only one he can love. . . . Pity for the woman whom the man loves less than she loves him becomes a terrifying passion.

No shade in Suarès' portrait, no restriction to his unbounded admiration. He composes his novels with a splendid organic order; he is "the least barbaric of artists," Suarès repeats in *Présences*. He is not, of course, an apostle of art for art's sake, but of art for the sake of God. Through his writings, he inspires all men with a divine love. If he is obscure in his passionate discussion of the ultimate philosophical problems, let us proclaim, asserts the Frenchman, "that obscurity is the most beautiful thing in the world, and that nothing in art is more valuable than such darkness." In the years when the Russian Revolution filled many a Frenchman with fear and horror, Suarès cried out: "We must have faith in the Russian people, on account of Dostoevsky. . . . He is the most profound heart, the greatest conscience of the modern world" (*Présences*, p. 363). Copeau, reviewing those rapturous love declarations of Suarès to the Russian prophet-moralist, praised him for surrendering himself unreservedly to him. Too many timorous readers were, on the contrary, afraid to recognize themselves in the Russian novelist and found it reassuring to call him "a Slav" and all right for the Slavs. He preferred the enthusiasm of Suarès and that of Claudel. The latter had remarked in a conversation: "If it is a question of influence, how many will be *capable* of submitting to it?"[7]

A young admirer of Claudel and, for a time, of Gide had proved capable of seeking that influence and of bowing to it—Rivière's friend and later his brother-in-law, killed at twenty-eight at the beginning of World War I, Alain-Fournier. He had been drawn to none of the novelists of France, except, and only for a time and on account of his flamboyance, to Barrès. He had evinced hardly more attraction toward the novelists of Britain, although he had made

English literature his special field of study and had spent some months in England. Poetry had been his, and Rivière's, passion while they were in college. He carried within himself the lingering nostalgia for a girl whom he felt convinced he had loved at first sight, would forever love, and would conjure up as the dreamt of and angelic woman whom his double, the Grand Meaulnes, would pursue and lose. Then, in March 1909, he confided to Rivière that he had just received the revelation of Dostoevsky's *The Idiot*. He was suddenly as powerfully impressed as he had been earlier by the discovery of Claudel. In that novel, he explained, he was seeking and finding a subtle and profound emotion, a sixth sense, as it were, which he called "the tact of the soul":

> That aperception of the soul, very sudden, has something, at times, frightening and repulsive. But then that infinite delicacy with which it is approached draws tears of blood. To that gift Myshkin owes his secret, not for explaining everything, for he explains nothing, but for making "everything explicable" through his sole presence.[8]

He continued reading and rereading the novel and, on May 20, 1909, he confided to Rivière that *The Idiot* had brought him close to what both of them called "the Christian temptation." The novel is in no way that of a converter; religion is hardly mentioned in it. Nevertheless, he added, "that book may well be the bridge for which I have long yearned, between the Christian world and my own." Through a curious coincidence, Alain-Fournier, in 1910-11, became, in Paris, the tutor of a young American who was then conceiving a poem that was later to become famous: "The Love Song of J. Alfred Prufrock." When an American critic, J. C. Pope, brought out in an ingenious article in *American Literature* (17, No. 3, Nov. 1945), the striking parallels between Prufrock and Raskolnikov and surmised that T. S. Eliot was probably reading Dostoevsky in Mrs. Garnett's translation, the poet corrected his commentator in a subsequent number (18, No. 4, Jan. 1947) of the same journal:

> I have never read Mrs. Garnett's translation of *Crime and Punishment*. The poem of Prufrock as conceived some time in 1910.

... During the period of my stay in Paris [in 1910–11], Dostoevsky was very much a subject of interest amongst literary people
and it was my friend and tutor, Alain-Fournier, who introduced
me to this author. Under his instigation, I read *Crime and Punishment, The Idiot* and *The Brothers Karamazov* in the French translation during the course of that winter. These three novels made a
profound impression upon me and I had read them all before
"Prufrock" was completed.

Alain-Fournier remained fascinated and disturbed by those Russian novels, so different from the one he was carrying inside him and
then attempting to write during those years 1909–12. In July 1911,
again he mentioned to Rivière how moved he was by *The Raw
Youth* (the French title is *L'Adolescent*) and the struggle between
crime and salvation in that short novel, the terrifying figure of
Arcady, and the towering character of Versilov. Then his own life
became engulfed in an emotional turmoil and, if Dostoevsky did not
lead him to an unreserved acceptance of Christianity, the young
admirer of *The Idiot* was not free from his obsession with the Russian when death sought him out soon after the battle of the Marne,
where his friend Péguy, he, too, a near-convert, had perished.[9]

The six or seven years that followed World War I were in France,
as in Germany and to a lesser extent in Britain, a time of widespread
enthusiasm for Dostoevsky and, through him, for a certain idea of
the "Slavic soul," such as had not been seen in Western Europe and
has not been witnessed since. The Russian emigration in those years
contributed much to the fashion for things Slavic, in food, drink,
entertainment, clothes, music, and books. It gave French literature
several novelists and essayists of note. Its intellectual and political
long-range effects have not yet been appraised in any thorough study.
For a while, it seemed as if the French expected every Russian émigré
to behave like a character from "The White Nights" or from *The
Demons,* just as in 1944–45 they looked upon every G.I. as a devotee
of William Faulkner or of Joseph Steinbeck. Some of those Russian
émigrés did their very best to warn the French that Dostoevsky was
not Russia, and certainly not all of Russia. They insisted that other
storytellers were far more representative of their country, insofar as

such a vast and contradictory country could ever be reduced to one interpretation. Vladimir Nabokov has done his utmost, in paradoxical and mocking terms, to warn the French first, then the Americans, that Dostoevsky should not be considered as an artist, but as "a prophet, a clap-trap journalist and a slapdash comedian." He repeated that he personally, and many other Russians, could not bear "his sensitive murderers and soulful prostitutes."[10] He advised Europeans and Americans to abandon that absurd cult and to venerate Gogol instead.

Other Russians urged their French friends to prefer Chekhov, or Leskov, or almost any other novelist to the distorted image of Russia that they were receiving from *The Idiot* and *The Gambler*. A Russian émigré in Paris, who became one of the shrewdest French writers on the theater and on the ballet in the first decade after 1918, André Levinson, multiplied essays on other Russian authors, in whom he attempted to interest French readers. His success was only moderate. Another critic who made himself an eloquent and highly competent intermediary between Slavic and Gallic men of letters was Vladimir Pozner. He resorted to the sharpest weapon, ridicule, to explode the myth of "the Slavic soul" as seen through Dostoevsky. Behind the loudly proclaimed admiration of the French for Myshkin or Kirilov, he sensed not a little complacency: the French admired a monster all the more wildly, and safely, for his being foreign and "an Easterner." Moreover, he was an epileptic, and several of his characters are too. *Ergo,* a crazy author produces crazy works for the complacent enjoyment of the rational Westerners who occasionally take a holiday from their innate wisdom and watch the antics of those Russian cuckolds, buffoons, and assassins.

In a scathing article published on June 26, 1926, in *Les Nouvelles littéraires,* Pozner mocked those French stories that had turned fashionable in the early twenties in which vaguely Slavic characters indulged in "gratuitous acts," behaved unpredictably, gulped vodka while devouring caviar without knife or fork, and discussed God until the small hours. Imagining Russia from a reading of Dostoevsky's fiction, he warned the French, was exactly as if one pictured Denmark through *Hamlet,* Crete through Racine's *Phèdre,* and Italy through *Romeo and Juliet.* Pozner himself stood second to none in his admiration for the Russian novelist as an artist and as a portrayer of character. He praised him for offering a unique "slow motion picture of accelerated feelings" and for depicting the enacting of the unconscious urges that lurk in every one of us. But he declared it absurd for his French admirers to transfigure him into a prophet of universal love and an evangelical saint. More than the "religion of suffering" by which Vogüé had epitomized Dostoevsky's message, there was in him a "volupté sadique de la souffrance." A smell of corruption and of death is exhaled by his crucial scenes, as by Zoshima's corpse, over which Western devotees of the Russian were piously and naively pouring perfume.

Such warnings however proved of little avail while the enthusiasm of the French ran high. The very same André Levinson had to yield to the expectation of the public and of the publishers and to write *La Vie pathétique de Dostoevsky* (Plon, 1931), to this day as vibrant a biography of the novelist as exists in French, though less detailed than a later one by another Russian-born writer, Henri Troyat (Fayard, 1940); the latter enjoyed the advantage of utilizing biographies in languages other than French, such as the one by Avrahm Yarmolinsky, published in New York (Harcourt Brace) in 1934. A Russian religious thinker who, without espousing either Catholicism or French citizenship, came very close to matching the prestige of Jacques Maritain and of Simone Weil with the French public, Nicholas Berdiaev, wrote a fervent interpretation of Dostoevsky's theodicy and philosophy, which was widely read in France and appeared in English in 1934 (New York: Sheed and Ward).

Heads had remained cooler across the Channel. A very young man, who became subsequently an uneven, but occasionally shrewd, critic (and Katherine Mansfield's husband), John Middleton Murry, had brought out, even before the Russian Revolution of 1917, a volume on Dostoevsky (London: Martin Secker, 1916) in which enthusiasm knew no bounds. "He is a power whose influence may well be incalculable, not upon the form, but upon the thought and spirit of our literature. . . . The Russian thought which shall renew humanity found its most perfect expression in Dostoevsky's novels"—such was the tone of his introductory chapter. Constance Garnett had provided the British public with adequate translations of Dostoevsky's works between 1905 and 1920. Her husband was an influential man of letters, and he saw to it that the best known English writers receive some at least of the translated works. Their reaction was a guarded one. It has been summarized in the excellent study by Helen Muchnic, first presented as a thesis at Bryn Mawr College and later published in the *Smith College Studies in Modern Languages,* 20 (April and July 1939), 3–4—*Dostoevsky's English Reputation (1881–1936).* Joseph Conrad was among those who did not conceal their aversion: "It's an impossible lump of valuable matter. It's terrifically bad and impressive and exasperating. . . . I do know that he is too Russian for me" (after a reading of *The Brothers Karamazov*). Henry James wrote to Hugh Walpole on May 18, 1912, that he clung to form above all, as the one safeguard "from the welter of helpless verbiage that we swim in as in a sea of tasteless tepid pudding." Both Tolstoy and Dostoevsky suffered incurably, in his eyes, from the grave vice that was "their lack of composition, their defiance of economy and architecture." "What incoherence and verbiage," exclaimed John Galsworthy after a second reading of *The Brothers Karamazov,* and he went on, in a letter to the translator's husband, Edward Garnett, on April 15, 1914, "It's a mark of these cubistic, blood-bespattered-poster times that Dostoevsky should rule the roost." D. H. Lawrence, though he belonged to a younger generation and to another social class, declared the moral scheme of those Russian novelists "dull, old, dead." To Lady Ottoline Morrell, he wrote even more frankly:

> I have been reading Dostoevsky's *Idiot.* I don't like Dostoevsky. He is again like the rat, slithering in hate, in the shadows, and, in order to belong to the light, professing love, all love.

He found *The Demons* even more repulsive, dirty, and degrading. Petronius, by comparison, was "straight and above board. . . . But Dostoevsky, mixing god and sadism, he is foul." Later he relented somewhat in his opposition, but he never altered his fundamental position of intense dislike.

Helen Muchnic, from whom these quotes are borrowed, entitles her chapter on the years 1912-21 "The Dosteoevsky Cult." It was indeed. Several English fiction writers who came after, like Somerset Maugham and V. S. Pritchett, have drawn a more dispassionate balance sheet of the impact of the Russian novelist. Pritchett, in *The New Statesman* of November 16, 1962, joked about the passing of the vogue of "the Russian soul," which, he hints, Dostoevsky "invented out of the Svengali side of his nature." The potion thus concocted by the novelist had intoxicated the West in the twenties. Dostoevsky had expected Russia to save the West, beginning with the occupation of Constantinople. Then the Bolsheviks took over the mission of salvation. They undertook to make the U.S.S.R. efficient, and they repudiated Dostoevsky. Still, adds the ironical critic,

> . . . when we saw Krushchev banging his shoe, we recalled that Stavrogin once bit a governor's ear; when we watched the Russian trials, we thought of Lebedev caught in the sin-confession cycle or of Mitya Karamazov, of whom Dostoevsky wrote. "His soul accepts punishment, not because he has committed the crime of which he will be accused, but because he is wicked enough to be capable and desirous of committing it." He is a thoroughly Russian character.

V. S. Pritchett refused however to be taken in by the glib generalization that points to Dostoevsky as providing the key to the secrets of the Russian soul. He preferred to stress the comic and dramatic genius of the novelist, even though his "laughter sounds hyena-like." Even his much vaunted contradictions are comic, "for he brought histrionic excess to them."

In contrast, if the French had a fault, as Sterne hinted in another context, they were too serious. Many of them fell for the conventional generalizations about the Slavic soul and the regeneration (or the degeneration) of the Latin spirit through Dostoevsky. But they also admired the artist in him. One of the least reserved in his praise was a medical doctor who was one of the greatest writers on art of his generation and its greatest lyrical critic, Élie Faure. No French Calvinist was ever more wildly romantic, readier to vibrate unrestrainedly in the presence of beauty, and a wilder life-worshipper than he. He was born in 1873, not long after Gide, Proust, and

Valéry, and he deserves to rank not far from them as an artist in prose. The first of his many volumes in which he truly came into his own as a thinker was *Les Constructeurs* (1921). He collected in it essays on the great men who had molded him and the men of his own age—Lamarck, Nietzsche, Michelet, Cézanne, and Dostoevsky. The latter is celebrated in hyperbolic tones, as a man great throughout his wretchedness, as an artist, but chiefly as a prophet of love that is essentially charity and of which the weary, self-doubting West stands in need in order to effect its rejuvenation. The tone is declamatory; lofty metaphors, imperious aphorisms, delirious exclamations abound. Yet the critic does not fail to perceive the architecture of those novels, so different from the simpler, unilinear French ones, and to celebrate the sensuality and carnal reality from which springs the spirituality of Dostoevsky, that "Aeschylus of modern fiction." Throughout the thirty volumes that he feverishly composed while practising as a doctor, until death carried him away in 1937, Élie Faure was to echo some of the ethical and aesthetic teachings that he had received, early in his career, from the Russian novelist.

Little is known of the circumstances and the manner in which Proust discovered Dostoevsky. He must, however, have mentioned him in his conversation and have impressed his friends with some precise knowledge of his novels since, in 1921, the centenary of Dostoevsky's birth, the director of the *Nouvelle Revue française,* Rivière, asked Proust to write an article on him. Proust was then too concerned with completing his long work to agree to Rivière's request. He modestly remarked that he knew the Russian novelist only imperfectly. But it is clear from random allusions in his works that he was familiar with the four great novels and at least with the *Memories from the House of the Dead,* the first volume composed after the prisoner's return from Siberia.

Proust expressed himself twice on Dostoevsky in ways other than mere passing allusions: in an undated two-page essay, probably written a few months before his death in November 1922, now included in *Contre Sainte-Beuve* (posthumously published in 1954), and in striking pages in *La Prisonnière,* also posthumously published, which are most conveniently found in the third volume of the

Pléiade edition of *A la Recherche* (pp. 376 ff). The first passage asserts, without elaborating on the point, that the novelist's originality lies primarily in his composition. In it, Proust also surmises that there must have occurred a criminal act somewhere in the novelist's life (as several of Dostoevsky's contemporaries hinted or averred) and that he had his fictional creatures commit that crime; he accepted the punishment for it. It has since been remarked more than once that the occasional German rendering of the title as "Sin and Redemption" would be truer to the spirit of Dostoevsky's most famous novel than the French or the English title.

The other passage is familiar to readers of Proust. In it, he clearly expressed some ideas that were dear to him. They occur in the volume in which Marcel holds Albertine captive, relishes and probes his jealousy and his anguish, and occasionally endeavors to instruct her. Those pages are a digression that Proust must have felt important. Marcel has just asked Albertine to play Vinteuil's sonata for him; he reflects on how slow is, and probably must be, the progressive deciphering of a masterpiece by posterity. He alludes to two novels of Thomas Hardy, which Albertine presumably had read, to Stendhal, to Vermeer. His point, to which Proust often returned, was that great writers and artists have never composed anything but one work under varied guises; they have been the mirrors of only one beauty. Such had been the case for Dostoevsky. His women all belong to the same type, physically and psychologically. They all have the same way of passing from mysterious capriciousness to dreadful insolence. The houses in which crucial events take place in *Crime and Punishment,* in *The Idiot,* and in *The Brothers Karamazov* all have an air of similarity, as have the houses and the rooms in the different paintings by Ver Meer.

Shyly, Albertine then questions her mentor on the obsession with crime in those novels. She wonders, as many another reader must have done, whether that obsession betrayed a shameful deed that the author might have committed. Marcel cannot say for sure. But he concedes that the Russian novelist must have known sin, like most of us, in some forbidden shape. Moreover, imaginative creators are tempted by crimes, monstrosities, or merely by urges not necesarily acted upon. Most striking in Dostoevsky, he insists, is the juxtaposition of opposite feelings, as if love and most rabid hatred, shyness and gross insolence, were but two facets of the same personality. Proust singled out some of the most hair-raising scenes in *The Brothers Karamazov* (the poor, crazy woman whom old Karamazov has gotten with child having her delivery in the garden of the old man, as if she served as the passive tool of vengeful destiny; her son, Smerdiakov, murdering his lecherous father, then hanging himself) to compare with the most august art works by Rembrandt or by Italian sculptors.

Is it possible to assign any actual influence on Proust's novelistic technique to his reading of Dostoevsky? It would be rash to do so, since the very tone in which that digression on the Russian novelist is written and its position in the latter part of the long saga-novel (other allusions occur in the very last volumes) suggest that Proust read Dostoevsky after the organization of his work, when his psychological and aesthetic views had already been reached. Proust, spontaneously, had chosen a presentation of his characters that was to throw his readers on the wrong track, then confuse them again, and only then would the complex truth be revealed to them. Proust must have felt, when he pored over the Russian novelist, that he was confirmed in his own instinctive conception of character, which allowed for the sudden appearance of totally unexpected feelings and for the emergence of a different person (a double or an altogether different personality) in some character. He also found himself justified by the example of his Russian predecessor in his own method of taking up similar situations or similar scenes over and over again and in his didactic digressions, which he called "intellectual passages interpolated into the narrative." To be more precise and to attempt to locate specific influence would be far fetched and would result in distorting the Proustian process of composition.[11]

The French novelists of a younger generation than that of Gide and Proust, born, as was Alain-Fournier, in the middle 1880's (Mauriac, Duhamel, Bernanos) or even fifteen years later (Julien Green, Malraux, perhaps even Arland and Drieu La Rochelle), proved more receptive to the impact of Dostoevsky than their British counterparts, or more willing to acknowledge it. Mauriac has often been hailed, by the more traditional French critics, as the novelist of his age group who upheld the banner of classical fiction (that of Balzac and Flaubert). He was praised by them for having carried over Racinian tragedy, condensed, unilinear, feverish, into the craft of fiction. His novels are indeed brief, tragically tense; they allow little scope for the swarming of episodes and the philosophical or political dissertations. None of them may be asserted to bear the imprint of Dostoevsky or, for that matter, of any of the nineteenth-century French or English masters of fiction. But he, the least cosmopolitan of French novelists of his age group, nevertheless reflected on his art. He did so, fortunately, after he had produced several of his best works and not just to plead for his own vision and his own technique. In those reflections he did not conceal what an enrichment to the art of fiction in general and to his own conception of his craft Dostoevsky had brought.

In 1928, in a slim volume given to a new collection of *Cahiers de la Quinzaine,* published as "L'Artisan du livre," *Le Roman,* he contrasted, as Gide had done, but with more fairness to his French predecessors of the nineteenth century, Balzac and Dostoevsky. Balzac, he comments, explained Grandet, or Goriot, or Baron Hulot, or Claës through his ruling passion, his monomania. His bent was to impose an order upon nature and to stress the coherence of the characters, controlled by a logic that was at times forced upon them by the novelist's vision. He reached profound truths on human nature thereby. But another novelist appeared, who shied away from introducing a preconceived order or logic into the psychology of his creatures. He made them "not beings of reason, . . . but of flesh and bones, loaded with inherited burdens, capable of almost anything in good or evil." All of us since, Mauriac submits, have been marked by Dostoevsky. His heroes may, at first, strike a Frenchman as weird. But that is not because they are Russian, but because each of us is like them, a living chaos, moved by the logic of life, which appears like sheer illogic to would-be rational Frenchmen.

We would like to forget that we are not very different from those Slavic beings; but if we are honest with ourselves we have to take in those new truths and, Mauriac contends, blend them with our own fiction. Dostoevsky's illogic and indeterminacy may very well become wedded to the more traditional qualities of the French novel.[12]

Again, Mauriac asserted that need for the French novel to broaden itself thanks to the example of the Russians in *Le Romancier et ses personnages* (Corrêa, 1933). Despite his immense admiration for Proust repeatedly proclaimed, he voiced the regret that none of the Proustian creatures ever knew moral anguish, moral scruples, remorse, or strove for perfection. The work of Dostoevsky proved superior to *A la Recherche* because it did encompass a Christian dimension and depicted prostitutes and criminals as fallen, but also as redeemed.

Much later, in January 1959, when Mauriac indulged in reminiscing on his youth, he recalled how as a teenager he had purchased in Bordeaux a copy of Dostoevsky's *A Raw Youth (L'Adolescent),* hoping he would find in it an answer to his own torments. But he was repelled by the first chapters and, seized with shame, he burnt the book in his fireplace: "That was my first encounter with Dostoevsky. It was I who was the great Inquisitor, I, the child lighting that pyre." Then, rereading the celebrated parable of the Inquisitor at seventy-five, he found himself fascinated again by the Russian novelist, "one of the gods of my youth, from whom I had grown somewhat remote." He adds:

> In literature, I was always afraid of drawing too near madness, especially when religion comes into play. I do not like that the portico opening on unknown eyes be epilepsy. . . . Yet the epileptic reasons. He is eminently reasonable. . . . He answers the anguish distilled by atheism. He was the herald of the godless world which came into being after he died and whose banner is now going to be planted on other planets.

Julien Green, more disturbed inwardly, more desperately in need of what he considered a harmonious French balancing of his diverse legacies (American South, Protestant training, attraction to Catholicism, lure of Buddhist mysticism), confessed in April 1949, in the fifth volume of his *Journals* (published at Plon in 1951), that he had consistently refused to read Dostoevsky. Then, at nearly fifty years of age, he bought at last an English version of *Crime and Punishment.* One year later, on May 27, 1950 (volume VI of his *Journals,* Plon, 1955, pp. 5, 82), he jotted down his reaction to that book. He was overwhelmed, and he remained in that state. He knew then that he had been well advised to keep away from him, and he approved of Joseph Conrad for having done likewise: "An instinctive, and perfectly legitimate jealousy it was. . . . If I had read him earlier, a whole part of my work would have been different." He was put off, however, by *The Idiot,* and he could not bring himself to believe in that novel. He, who has not a drop of French blood in him, missed logic and clarity in those disconcerting characters, suddently coming into a big legacy or throwing banknotes wildly into the fireplace. He concluded, shifting to *Man and Servant,* that he much preferred Tolstoy to Dostoevsky, whom the French had overpraised.

George Bernanos has more than once been likened by his French admirers to Dostoevsky. French of the French he was, and even a very provincial Frenchman, although born in Paris and of very remote Spanish origin on his father's side. He never was drawn to foreign literatures, and the education he received was hardly literary. Born in 1888, profoundly attached to the Catholic traditions of medieval France and with much of the knight and of the Crusader in him, he was impressed by World War I and the dreary slaughter in the trenches. He was already close to forty when, in 1926, he broke into the world of letters with *Sous le Soleil de Satan.* There, and in *L'Imposture* (1928), and less felicitously in his attempt at writing a detective novel of some sort with *Un Crime* (1935), affinities may be detected between the world conjured up by the French novelist and that of Dostoevsky's fiction. The atmosphere is one of violence, with murders committed by disturbed teenagers who are marked for grace as well as for sin and are eventually seized with repentance. Human creatures are afflicted with original sin more conspicuously than in the Russian novels; they put to mistaken usage the gift, or the burden, of free will, as in Dostoevsky. Their drama is a spiritual conflict between their temptation to sin and the blandishments of grace, which they endeavor to deserve. The forces of evil in the human creature are personified by Satan, whose ubiquitous presence in Bernanos' novels is far more tangibly convincing than in the make-believe pseudo-Dostoevskian episode in Gide's *Faux-Monnayeurs.* Both novelists proclaim their detestation of pride as the unforgivable flaw; arrogantly at times, they celebrate the greatness of humility, and even of the humiliation of the self corroded by masochism. Both seem to assert the universal guilt of all creatures and to grant, in their theology, a larger role to Satan than to the Redeemer.[13]

Those are similarities of temperament, far stronger than the differences that separate the French Catholic from the Russian opponent of Catholicism, the militant Bernanos, who refused to bow to defeat, from the creator of Prince Myshkin. Both lived their ideas with passionate ardor and embodied them in their characters, to whom they generously lent vibrant ideological digressions. The atmosphere of their novels is often equally lurid, and ominous with tragic threats. With all the turgid vituperations and polemical wrath in their novels (Bernanos caricatured Anatole France in his first novel and André Gide in his last one, *Monsieur Ouine*), those two fictional worlds are illuminated by a halo of saintliness and the presence of the supernatural behind the tales of murder and of suicide. At times, when conjuring up the purity of childhood and denouncing the supreme crime, which is to offend children, Bernanos hits upon lapidary statements that recall those of his Russian predecessor: "To hate one's own species in oneself, is not that Hell?" (*L'Imposture*), which almost parallels the famous cry of *The Brothers Karamazov:* "Hell is the impossibility of loving." However, had the French novelist, about whose reading and literary tastes we know next to nothing, been actually impressed by *Crime and Punishment* or by *The Idiot* when he composed his visionary novels? It is hardly likely. Once again, to the much too precise and dangerously misleading concept of influence, that of an affinity between creators with a similar imagination should be preferred.

André Malraux wrote a penetrating review of *L'Imposture* in the *Nouvelle Revue française* of March 1928, which constitutes one of his most pregnant pronouncements on the art of fiction and on the creative process in general. Several of his remarks in praise of that "novel of intensity" might have been said by him of Dostoevsky. He is himself, next to Bernanos, the French novelist with whom the impressive name of the Russian has been linked most frequently. Dostoevsky is the novelist whose example is most often quoted in

Malraux's scattered reflections on the art of fiction, on Goya, and on other painters. We know, from the statements of those who were born around the dawn of the century, such ar Marcel Arland, how close to the characters in *The Demons* or to the "underground man" the young men in those years 1920–24 felt, parading their "nouveau mal du siècle" and their nihilism. In 1953, adding an incidental note to a small volume, *Malraux par lui-même* (Seuil), in which Gaëtan Picon was offering a picture of his personality, Malraux remarked that for forty years Dostoevsky's presence had been an overwhelming one on French novelists. The French, however, had not gone to him for models, but rather to George Eliot and to Tolstoy. Malraux's own admiration for Tolstoy is unbounded, as is his passionate cult of Stendhal. But the atmosphere of his novels (of the first three in particular), their themes of violence, eroticism, control over others, and their obsession with omnipresent death make those tense, jerky, imperious stories full of metaphysical implications the only ones in French, along with those of Bernanos, that come near Dostoevsky's creations.

As with the Russian, psychological analysis divorced from action and pursued for its own sake, long dear to a certain French fictional tradition, is eschewed. Malraux indulges in fewer digressions than do Dostoevsky's bulky, rambling novels; still, many of the actors, while deeply involved in action, seem to be there to voice and to discuss ideas. They are seldom as passive as some of the Russian ones and not at all inclined to humiliate themselves. They want to be heroic and to throw a challenge to the forces of fate and to death. They are often haunted with urges to kill as Dostoevsky had depicted; in their case, it stems from a desire to commit the supremely exalted act and to march along the one irreversible path. Thus Chen, in *La Condition humaine,* recalls Raskolnikov and the suicidal obsession of Kirilov. The nightmares of the solitary prisoners (Kyo, Katow, or the protagonist in *Le Temps du mépris*) conjure up very "Dostoevskian" visions of crawling insects. There are also similarities between the scenes of torture and the sadistic questioning of prisoners by ironical police officers in the two authors. Still, the characters in Malraux, even when they happen to be Orientals, Russians, or international adventurers who have flocked to Asia, never divest themselves of their Western mentality—they yearn for action for action's sake. They feel no urge for grace, for salvation; they do not particularly yearn for a belief in God, so that they may bear life without killing themselves, as do the monomaniacs in *The Demons*. The notion of sin is alien to them. To the undeniable affinities with Dostoevsky's world, there has been added an even more potent fascination in Malraux's characters and in the ethical quest of their creator—that of Nietzsche.[14]

To many Frenchmen, the tragic and ludicrous buffoons of Dostoevsky seem to hold a very special appeal; they probably impress them as peculiarly foreign, and Russian. Their antics, performed with a lack of reserve and of self-respect that upsets the self-righteous stress on honor of the Western Europeans, entertain the French as exotic clowns might do. Proust alone, among the twentieth-century French novelists, except at times Sartre, has been masterly enough to include comic scenes and to express a comic vision in his fiction. Mauriac, Bernanos, Green appear unwilling to relieve the tragic tension of their feverish novels in that way. Céline is a master of gross comic effects, but they differ fundamentally from the essentially charitable laughter of Dostoevsky, a novelist for whom he confessed his dislike.[15]

Malraux, however, has brought to life such a character, at once a buffoon striving to entertain others and himself and a mythomaniac with a compulsive need to lie. His behavior at the roulette, on the night when he should have tipped off his friend Kyo to his imminent arrest, his playful affection and showy generosity when he converses with the prostitute, his dread of his own sense of guilt are features that call to mind several of the buffoons in the novels of the Russian writer. But those antics seem somehow more contrived, more intellectually calculated to provide some relief between two scenes of tragedy. They amused his creator probably more than they do many of his readers; he was in fact so taken up by that comico-tragic character, apparently modelled from real life, that he had to eliminate from *La Condition humaine* a long erotic episode in which Clappique appeared as the duped clown. His obstrusive presence would have filled a whole section of the novel at a time when the tragic suspense could not well be prolonged overmuch. More than thirty-five years later, Malraux returned to Clappique and allowed him to fill in a whole chapter of his *Antimémoires* (1967).

Malraux has consistently kept shy of any revelations about his youth, his training, his reading, and even his tastes in art, although the latter can easily be surmised from his frequent writings on painting and sculpture. This was not an attempt on his part to hide his sources. He is proud enough, and great enough, to realize that he does honor to those from whom he may have borrowed. Besides, his personality is so rich and so imperious that it transmutes into his own gold whatever coins he may have borrowed. The names of Balzac, Stendhal, and Dostoevsky—the latter especially—recur most insistently in the few statements that he has made on his art. Those are elliptic remarks, often obscure or too casual to be woven by the critic into a body of considered opinions on the Russian novelist. But they show a long familiarity with the four long novels of Dostoevsky and much reflection on his technique.

The longest such pronouncements occur in Picon's *Malraux par lui-même* (Seuil, 1953). One of them (p. 41) deals with the complex counterpoint of Dostoevsky's creation and with the choir of his buffoons, "asking his heroes the eternal question: why did God create us?" Other equally pregnant interrogations ask how much, or how little, we know Dostoevsky's character, or about the springs of character creation in the Russian novelist or in Balzac, and about the imaginative process more generally (pp. 48, 58, 60). Dostoevsky is consistently ranked by Malraux close to Aeschylus or to Shakespeare. It is probably in part from meditating on his works that Malraux declares (p. 66): "The modern novel is, in my eyes, a privileged means of expression of the tragic in man, and not an elucidation of the individual."

In *Les Voix du Silence,* Malraux again refers to Dostoevsky in his ponderings over what he terms "the creative process." The Russian novelist serves to strengthen a favorite assertion of the critic: that a novelist is controlled by certain initial schemes or frameworks, and those, in their turn, alter the narratives that they have not provoked. Pity upon the novelist for whom the novel would be only a narrative exclaims Malraux. That statement is essential to an understanding of Malraux's own technique, as the best volume on Malraux's fictional technique, by Jean Carduner (Nizet, 1968), has skillfully demonstrated. The novel's function is to "mettre en scène," that is, to render present to the reader, and to dramatize, scenes. It does not have to narrate or to relate, but "to represent," that is, to make present to us what was in the past; of that art, Dostoevsky is the unchallenged master, for his novels are a feverish, breathtaking succession of scenes. The plot itself matters little. *La Condition humaine* and *Espoir* likewise are made up of expertly selected tragic scenes more or less linked by a narrative that is almost immaterial. As in Dostoevsky, scenes of talk and of reflection are inextricably mixed with scenes of dramatic action. As in Dostoevsky again, the setting is very carefully selected, never left to chance: the courtyard of a school in which the prisoners await death in the boilers of the locomotives, the lighting or the night effects in *Espoir*. Malraux remarked that Dostoevsky appears to start, like Balzac, from a square or from a room where he lies in wait for his characters to erupt, like fate spying upon mortals. In the first version of *The Idiot*, not Rogojin, but Myshkin himself was to be the murderer. The change then effected altered the character and the plot, but hardly the significance of the scene. Malraux has no difficulty in adducing analogies from the realm of artistic creation. His meditations on Dostoevsky reinforced those that he has made most of his life on the mystery of genius and on its function—to triumph over destiny. In what is probably his least controversial volume of philosophy of art, *Saturne, Essai sur Goya* (Pléiade, 1950), Malraux drew a suggestive parallel between those two creators, both set apart from mankind by something incurable (deafness in the case of Goya), both become prophets:

> Dostoevsky's novels turn into a predication; full of darkness and urgency, like all the languages of a modern prophet. And what is a prophet, but a man who addresses himself to other men, so as to rend their veil of blindness, to tear them away from the world of appearances and to offer them the world of his own truth?

The very few novels written in the 1920's that would seem to have made use of the clichés made fashionable by the Dostoevsky wave of that era were not composed by authors who might be said to have been of a Dostoevskian cast of mind; still less did they harbor what Nietzsche might have called "a chaos in their souls." They were by gently ironical and compassionate men, whom the slaughter of the trenches and the outburst of hatred that had seized the intellectuals of the nations at war had uprooted from their prewar faith in reason and progress. One of them, Georges Duhamel, had watched suffering closely, and not passively, as a doctor in, or very near, the trenches. They were not mystical enough to throw themselves into the "religion of suffering" or to hope outright for a regeneration of the Western world through either Buddha or Christ. It took a minimum of clear sightedness to realize that, for all its humility, Dostoevsky's message nowhere pointed to a lessening of the amount of sorrow in the world or to a bettering of social conditions. For one who, like Duhamel (and other medical doctors who turned to literature, Luc Durtain or Céline), had seen men blinded by bullets, maimed by machine guns, poisoned by gas, their brains damaged by shells, it would have sounded little short of inhuman, as it did later to the doctor in Camus' *La Peste,* to repeat that whatever plunges men into pain and sorrow is good for them and that the best lesson we can learn is that of humility. After the wave of uncritical enthusiasm that had catapulted Dostoevsky's novels forward around 1917-22, in part as the surest means of understanding the new Russian regime, the enlightened readers of the West came down to a saner view. The American expatriates in Paris deplored the fact that the Russian novelists lacked the humor or the aesthetic distance to make fun of themselves, as Sinclair Lewis and H. L. Mencken were beginning to do with acerbity. Virginia Woolf contemplated with some amusement those people who held what she called "the Russian point of view"; she suggested that we might offer to that queer, alien view of people and things more sympathy of the heart than sympathy of the mind. There was, of course, enough disturbance in herself and around her, in the Bloomsbury circle, for her to aspire after a gentler picture of her fellow beings.

Another sick person, soon to be attracted to a Russian form of soul treatment in Fontainebleau, Katherine Mansfield, was the wife of the young man whose rapturous biography of Dostoevsky had fed the enthusiasm of the British youth for the Russian, Middleton Murry. She treated Dostoevsky with affection and with amused condescension in an essay for the *Athenaeum* in 1919. It was harder for the French intellectuals to remain so detached, or so insular, after august writers, much respected by the emerging postwar youth, such as Gide, Suarès, Copeau, Faure had revered him in hyperbolic strains. In fictional works, however, they could picture a Dosto-evskian character, passive, athirst for humility, eager for suffering, discoursing unweariedly, consenting and almost desiring to be jilted by his wife, so that he might embrace her lover in the Russian fashion.

The most "Russian" character to whom Duhamel gave life is a typical Parisian of the lower middle class, a modest clerk in an office, such as Maupassant and the naturalist novelists of 1880–90 used to depict mercilessly. His name is Salavin. He has never head of Dostoevsky, probably not even of the Slavic soul and other common-places of the early 1920's. But he is grieved by the evil in the world, which he would like to cure or to lessen. He is no hero, no great brain; he has no talent, no leaning toward politics or social preach-ing, not even a religious faith. He realizes that he is a very ordinary man, and he decides one day to rise above his mediocrity and to acquire a new soul. He will become a saint. He studies in dictionaries the achievements of saints; to begin with, he must pursue humility. He looks for lepers to assist, ladies in distress to rescue, but finds few of those in Paris. He resolves to tell the truth bluntly, even, and especially, to those whom truth will hurt, so that they too may set out on the path to saintliness. He inflicts minor injuries to himself and stares at the grieved amazement of his puzzled wife. Naturally, he makes her miserable, his employer suspicious, he loses his job, and he has not even acquired the gift of charity or the true humility that might mean that he has received the blessing of grace.

The volume in which Duhamel has thus blended sympathy, humor, gentle satire is the third in his Salavin series, *Journal de Salavin* (1927). It has neither the depth nor the harrowing anxiety of Dostoevsky's stories, and Duhamel never displayed a powerful gift of inventiveness. He was most skillful at pleasant allegorical tales, in the polished manner of Anatole France, but with more warmth of sensibility; he sketched characters who were attractive, touching though seldom disturbing, projections of himself. Despite a few ventures into the depiction of humble, self-immolating, and invariably awkward people, he could not quite bring himself to believe in evil as a positive force in man or in the abrupt contradictions of tormented sinners. Soon after his Salavin cycle, which was completed with the fifth volume in 1932, Duhamel became an academician, a defender of traditional values of simplicity, clarity, naturalness, and a humanist who fought for moderation, wisdom, and order. The fanaticism of the Nazis, the self-incrimination of the Russians unjustly tried under Stalin, the cataclysms of 1940–44 left him bewildered and outraged. His novels, like those of Martin Du Gard or of Romains, were suddenly found not to be attuned to those tragic years. Dostoevsky, Faulkner, Malraux had proved to be the prophets of the lived apocalypse of violence and torture, not he.

One other novel of some distinction that bears the imprint of the Dostoevsky vogue and of the Russian clichés then prevalent, *L'Ecorché,* appeared the same year (1927) as *Journal de Salavin.* It received much less attention than it deserved and has never been translated into English. Its author was a Swiss writer of delicate talent, an able essayist and storyteller, Robert de Traz. It takes place in the Genevan middle class at a time when a number of Russians had established residence in the hospitable Swiss city. The hypersensitive unheroic hero, Marc, suffers from the minor jolts of life, or even from imaginary allusions, as if he were constantly flayed alive. He scorns himself voluptuously; realizing that he is endowed with neither courage nor willpower, he constantly humbles himself. He marries a Russian person who remains enigmatic, perhaps devoid of personality and of any capacity for affection, who does nothing but lie down, dream, smoke cigarettes, and discreetly scorn her lamentable husband. She gives shelter in their tiny apartment to a Russian Czarist ex-officer, who talks, drinks, and insults and threatens Marc, his host. The latter relishes his shame; now and then, he reasons that he should revolt and assert himself, but he vacillates in irresolution and remorse. At last, he is deserted by his Russian wife, who elopes with one of her bizarre, garrulous, and apparently irresponsible compatriots. The picture of the lamentable Genevan petty bourgeois, a Myshkin without saintliness and without any insight or an "underground man" complacently displaying his mediocrity, is done with verve and humor. The novel is skillfully built, in a traditional way. The sketches of the Russian exiles, proud of the mission of salvation assigned to their country by its prophetic novelist, ready to betray their hopeless cause in order to join the Red Army or the secret police of the Bosheviks, are entertaining. But nowhere does Robert de Traz come near the haunting vividness of his great Slavic predecessor.

It has been remarked more than once that by 1929–30, and not on account of political or economic events, the psychological and literary climate had been suddenly altered in Western Europe; a few discerning observers at the time were aware of it. In France, the new creative energy that had been released by the ending of World War I had spent itself. The hopes aroused by the reconstruction of a new Europe flagged, or were threatened. Russia was ceasing to appear to be the Messianic land from which a new dawn would irradiate toward the weary lands bordering the North Sea and the Atlantic. A number of pilgrims, confident that a new socialism was being built in Russia and that a spirit of fraternal "agapé" might prevail among the compatriots of Tolstoy and of Dostoevsky, traveled to Moscow and Leningrad, inquired about the literature and the social conditions in the country, and returned home disenchanted. They ceased to hope for a wind of charity and salvation blowing from the Slavic steppes. Political feuds and ideological debates raged in France as they did in Germany. The writers of a Catholic and traditionalist cast of thought voiced their fear of Russia as an Asiatic, nihilistic land and indicted Dostoevsky as a lover and teacher of chaos and of self-doubts. Those who sided with the Left denounced his reactionary views, his occasional anti-Semitic pronouncements, and looked to the postrevolutionary Russian writers as the more faithful portrayers of the new culture emerging in Eastern Europe.

The most influential volume on modern Russian letters was the *Panorama de la Littérature russe* by a Russian émigré, Vladimir Pozner (Kra, 1929); he devoted only two pages to Dostoevsky as one of the ancestors of the literature of the twentieth century. The author stressed the religion of pity and of universal love that might be read into *The Idiot* far less than the atmosphere of madness, crime, and sadism that fascinated his readers—in Russia, at any rate. The long chapter devoted to Dostoevsky in the most influential history of Russian literature for an English-speaking public, by D. S. Mirsky (1926), was decidedly cool to Dostoevsky. The Russian author and professor in England at that time underlined the novelist's partiality to sensationalism; he warned the supposedly gullible Western readers that the characters in Dostoevsky's fiction were no more representative of the real Russia of 1870-80 than the characters of *Wuthering Heights* were of Britain, or even of Yorkshire. In Russia, his influence had raged for a few years at the end of his career, then waned. The historian concluded (Ch. viii):

> Our organism has grown immune to his poisons, which we have assimilated and rejected. . . .The young men of today are not very far from placing him on a level with Dumas . . . .It would be wrong to lament that attitude; for the real Dostoevsky is food that is easily assimilated only by a profoundly diseased spiritual organism.

Dostoevsky's works were translated and easily available in the years 1929–39, read and discussed as classics, commented upon by scholars. Their appeal to younger creative writers had worn off. Malraux excepted, in the decade that preceded the Second World War, the French authors most influential with the general public were either precise, analytical intellects—Valéry, Romains, Sartre in the late thirties—unsympathetic to the Slavic chaos attributed to Dostoevsky, or Tolstoian sensibilities—Martin Du Gard, Giono, and other advocates of recovering a soothing harmony between man and nature. On the eve of the new upheaval in Europe, however, and during World War II, some words became current in literature, in journalism, and soon in everyday conversation that appeared to point to a new presence of Dostoevskian themes: absurdity, metaphysical suicide, universal responsibility, nihilism. The "subterranean man," as the French called him, became a stock allusion in ethical and philosophical essays. The *Notes from the Underground,* which in 1887 Nietzsche had read in the French version as *L'Esprit souterrain,* were currently linked with Kierkegaard, with Kafka's

*Metamorphosis,* and considered as a text throwing light on existentialism, of which Dostoevsky was made a forerunner.[16] The French writer of the new generation whose thought and writings are most closely linked with Dostoevsky is Albert Camus.

Once again, no question of influence on Camus' fiction arises. Like Gide, Camus knew that his gifts were those of a moralist, of an essayist, and of an author of typically French "récits," with no interweaving of plots and no swarming of characters. He was drawn to the theater. However, the conflicts that he staged were not dramatic ones, but rather the inner debates of the protagonists of *L'Etranger* and *La Chute* or the melancholy fights of two men of good will against the plague. His own pronouncements on the art of fiction point to his being fully aware of his position as a novelist—in the line of *La Princesse de Clèves* and of *Adolphe,* with the introspective classicists who clung to economy of means and to austere sparseness of style. Wisely, he never attempted a novel, or even a long short story, in the manner of the novelist whom he set above all others, Dostoevsky. The imaginative power of the great Russian fascinated him precisely because he realized that he could only keep respectfully at a distance from such an overflowing abundance, in the same way as other Frenchmen a century earlier, Baudelaire among them, had praised Balzac, Delacroix, or Hugo because those giants had possessed the power of a force of nature that had been denied to themselves.

Camus, modestly or proudly, frequently disassociated himself from his existentialist contemporaries and denied that he was a philosopher. He stood indeed, in that respect, closer to Malraux, who lived his own disconnected ideas with passion and never cared to organize what he might have borrowed from Nietzsche or Spengler into a synthesis, than to a systematic thinker like Sartre, whose successive contradictions were no less blatant, but of another sort. Dostoevsky was, in Camus' eyes, a philosopher-novelist, asking fundamental questions through his characters, and that stands at the opposite pole from being a novelist with a purpose. Of all the thinkers who may have provoked Camus into anguishing debates with himself (St. Augustine, Pascal, Hegel, Kierkegaard, Nietzsche), Dostoevsky was the one with whose characters he identified most unreservedly. At every stage of his meditations, he encountered him.

Young Camus must have read Dostoevsky's novels in translation early in his career, while he studied at the Lycée, then at the University in Algiers. In his early twenties, he had ambitiously attempted to stage Copeau's dramatic adaptation of *The Brothers Karamazov* (which had met with only moderate success in Paris at the Vieux Colombier in 1924 and in New York at the Theater Guild in 1927) at his Théâtre de l'Equipe. In *Le Mythe de Sisyphe,* which appeared in Paris in 1942, a section of Part III, "absurd creation," was entitled "Kirilov"; it was substituted for a chapter on Kafka, which was subsequently added as an appendix to the volume. Camus' meditation in that book had been set in motion, as it had in his own life after he had been apprised of his tubercular condition, by the confrontation with suicide, "the one really serious philosophical problem," as the opening sentence in the volume asserts. In his youthful, imperious way, through short, affirmative, and at times unconnected sentences, Camus recalls the constant interrogation of Dostoevsky's characters: what is the meaning of life? If life is altogether absurd, because faith in immortality is absent or ruled out, is not suicide the logical consequence? The Russian novelist had pondered the tragic question, both in his own meditations in *The Diary of a Writer* in 1876 and in *The Demons.* In the latter, Kirilov undertook to wreak his revenge upon nonexistent God and to assert his unbounded revolt through killing himself. His reasoning, Camus comments, has a classic clarity: "If God does not exist, Kirilov is God. If God does not exist, Kirilov must kill himself . . . in order to be God." The essence of his own godhead lies, in Kirilov's eyes, in his unlimited freedom. To kill God is, as it is for Nietzsche, "to become God oneself," to reach eternal life on this very earth.

Such logic appears insane to many. But Kirilov is a rival of Christ. In Dostoevsky's oft-quoted sentence, over which Camus and many French readers assiduouly meditated, "man only invented God so as to live without killing himself." To open the eyes of his fellow-beings, whose voluntary blindness amounts to cowardice, Kirilov will kill himself—for love of mankind. He feels *obliged* to immolate himself and to assert his freedom. That "absurd suicide" that fascinates Camus in his strange dialectics is pursued by Stavrogin in the same novel and later by Ivan Karamazov. Those assertions of Dostoevskian characters, Camus concedes (or proclaims, since he has bestowed a noble significance upon the adjective), are "absurd":

> But what prodigious creation is that, in which beings of fire and ice become familiar to us! The passionate world of indifference which thunders in their hearts in no way strikes us as monstrous. In it we find our own daily anguish. No one certainly has ever known as well as Dostoevsky how to endow the absurd world with such a torturing and, to us, such an intimate fascination.[17]

Camus was certainly spellbound by the reasoning of Kirilov or by that of Ivan. Early in his literary life he had spurned the belief in immortality as a cowardly abdication. He had vehemently denied that, for him at any rate, death could be merely a gate opening onto another life. He never shifted his position on that essential denial. Nor did he experience any trauma from the death of God. Although he found atheism a little vulgar and declined to profess it, as some existentialists were doing loudly around him, he, unlike Dostoevsky, was not obsessed with the problem of the existence or nonexistence of God. On several occasions, he repeated that the crucial question for the moderns was, as he saw it, to ponder over how man can behave when he believes neither in God nor in reason. What values are left standing for him who, like the hero of *L'Etranger* awaiting death in his prison cell, spurns the solace of the supernatural? Like many a reader of the novel, the author of *The Brothers Karamazov* himself seems to have been more impressed by the logic of Ivan in his denials of any justification for the suffering of innocent children, than by the novelist's attempt to counter that reasoning through the saintly faith of Alyosha. The chapter on Kirilov in the volume on Sisyphus remains inconclusive. The Russian novelist merely helped the French novelist express his own quandary over what he termed the absurd and his conviction that nobility for the human creature who had faced absurdity unflinchingly lay in revolting. And the work of art is the most valuable form of revolt, because it converts abstract reasoning into carnal and concrete terms.

There are Dostoevskian echoes in the last novel that Camus published (in 1956). The long, self-incriminatory, falsely humble monologue of the speaker has undertones of the ravings of the "underground man" laying bare his craving for being humiliated. *La Chute* is not only, as the author remarked, "the most anti-Christian of his books" and a satire on the garrulous men of letters (his former friends, the existentialists included) who merge and drown their own guilt into universal guilt. It is also a testimony to the bitterness of Camus who, after the polemics in which his former friends had torn to shreds his previous attempt at philosophy of history, reexamined himself mercilessly. Had he not, indeed, presented himself too favorably in some of his essays, played the complacent and at times pompous personage dispensing advice to his admirers, whom Dostoevsky had depicted? The bitter humor of Dostoevsky's buffoons held a strange fascination for him, as for many other French readers. Questioned once by an interviewer on which theme he considered as most obsessively present in his works, he answered "humor." That humor is often tinged with bitterness.[18]

The volume by Camus that had been the butt of the harshest criticism by Jeanson, Sartre, and not a few other reviewers when it appeared in 1951 is indeed a strangely uneven and disconnected one—*L'Homme révolté*. The author cannot but have been aware of it; hence the tone of self-laceration that is strident in *La Chute* and in Camus' most striking short story, "Le Renégat." The impact of Dostoevsky on Camus' reflection may have been in part responsible for the feeling of embarrassment that the book arouses in many readers. Again, the two characters around whom Camus' meditation centers are Kirilov and Ivan Karamazov. The latter sits in judgment on God and refuses to accept the very notion of divine creation, if evil must be a necessary element in that creation. He sets justice against grace. He will not bow to the facile argument that suffering is necessary for us to reach a higher truth. If such a truth exists, Ivan will spurn it, because it is unjust. He thus reaches the nihilistic conclusion that everything is allowed. He will perpetrate evil acts out of logical consistency. To Camus, who had advocated revolt as the one courageous course in the face of the absurdity prevailing in the universe, Ivan's reasoning led to the harrowing interrogation:

"Is it possible to go on living in the context of revolt?" Will Ivan, having denied God and immortality, consent that his father be murdered? He who revolted against the iniquitous suffering of innocent children is constrained by his logic to agree to a crime. With him, Camus concludes, "the revolt of reason ends in madness."

Other chapters of the same anguished, frequently enigmatic or confused volume revolve around the nihilists in Russian history, who made their mark at the time of *The Demons* and *The Brothers Karamazov*. In 1949, Camus had composed a drama, *Les Justes,* on a similar theme: the murder, in 1905, of an uncle of the Czar by a young terrorist who was sentenced to be hanged. The murderer wanted justice, and he committed a crime. The girl who assists him prophesies that others will come one day and will likewise kill, in the name of justice, but they will be acclaimed for it. The abstract problem was one that the French, around 1945–50, still fresh from their experience under Nazism and torn between the sight of Stalinist tyranny and the selfishness of American capitalism, were anxiously debating in their literature. But the problem and its ideological dilemmas preceded their carnal embodiment in a play and harmed it. That pseudo-Dostoevskian drama, with its abstract aphorisms and its purely theoretical problem, fails to come to life on the stage; in its tenseness and rigidity, it strikes the playgoer as artificial. When performed again in Camus' lifetime, and again in 1966 after his death, it appeared to critics and audiences as an incoherent and rhetorical play. The "theater of ideas" can be even more artificial than the "novel of ideas" that Camus himself had condemned. Perhaps any attempt to convert the long, complex novels of Dostoevsky into dramas must likeise end in disappointment.

Camus experienced it, after some others. The characters in a work of fiction may debate on what to do to their heart's content and impart their anguishing dilemmas to the reader. On the stage, we require the events themselves to face us directly. Camus' adaptation of the novel *The Demons* (he used the familiar, if less accurate, title *Les Possédés*) to the stage in 1959 remains cerebral and lofty. He has Kirilov, Stavrogin, and other male and female characters exchange neat, rhetorical aphorisms. However, their personalities remain sketchy and abstract to the onlooker. The intensity that

Camus had experienced in steeping himself in the original is not conveyed with a dramatic language of its own or in a gripping dramatic form. Much had to be eliminated for which the device of an ironical and somewhat exterior "narrator" (filling in the gaps and explaining the events) could not quite compensate. It proved a source of grief for a writer who had much warmth as a man and in his moralist's essays and whose lifelong interest had centered on the stage that he thus felt unable to shake off a certain coldness that froze his dramatic attempts.

The work that Camus did on the dramatic adaptation of that novel afforded him an opportunity to express himself on Dostoevsky more directly than he had done in his earlier books. His main statements have been collected at the end of the volume of his works in the Pléiade edition entitled *Théâtre, Récits, Nouvelles* (1963), pp. 1873-83. In Dostoevsky, he admired the profound probing into human nature, but also the prophetic genius who had, as Camus saw it, expressed, and actually lived, "our historical fate." He ranked *The Demons* in particular among the four or five greatest works of literature; he felt that the volume was even more meaningful and cogent to his own time than it might have been in the Russia of Dostoevsky:

> *Les Possédés* is a prophetic book, not only because they herald our nihilism, but because they present torn, or dead, souls, incapable of love and suffering from that inability to love, wanting to believe and unable to do so, the very same beings who today fill our own society and our spiritual world.

To a Russian visitor, to whom he had pointed out that two portraits alone adorned his study and inspired him, those of Tolstoy and Dostoevsky, Camus declared outright that "without Dostoevsky, twentieth century French literature would not have been what it was." To him Camus also confided that he had owed to Dostoevsky a genuine revelation when he first read him at twenty, and then again at forty. For the Russian novelist reveals to us what we are well aware of, but refuse to acknowledge. Long before anyone else, he had foreseen our contemporary nihilism and its monstrous consequences; he had also pointed the way to our salvation: "His tragic hope is to cure humiliation through humility, and nihilism through self-denial" (p. 1879). He had maintained that salvation could not be extended to all if the suffering of a single person were to be excluded from it. Camus ended that statement, which he delivered in 1955 on the radio, with the bold assertion: "Dostoevsky's greatness will not cease growing, for our world will either perish, or justify him to have been right. . . . He towers over our literatures and our history. Today he continues to help us live and hope."

Camus was modest, but probably right, when he disclaimed any ambition to be a philosopher. If to be one means thinking with logic and rigorous consistency or disguising one's contradictions under an imperious structure of assertions, Camus could not, any more than Valéry, Gide, or Malraux, lay claim to such a title. The vagueness of many of his views in *L'Homme révolté* and the frailty of much of his argumentation cannot be attributed to Dostoevsky's influence on his thought and sensibility. But he tensely lived his own contradictions, as the Russian novelist had probably done. And, lacking Dostoevsky's power to dramatize them and to *be* Ivan as well as Alyosha in deed or in passionate dialectics, Camus had to reason in a theoretical way; Dostoevsky had not done differently outside his fictional works, in his *Journals of a Writer,* for example. And he had fallen prey to similar weaknesses. Camus, advocating revolt and finding in it a source of fraternal love, preaching the awareness of absurdity as a boon and deriving a strange optimism from it, proclaiming his fascination with Dostoevsky's excesses and at the same time his attachment to a Hellenic sense of measure, may well appear to be a bundle of contradictions. The controversy that his volume on revolt brought about embittered him. André Breton was irate against Camus because he appeared to have written slightingly of Lautréamont, the sacred cow of the surrealists; disapproving of the novel for general reasons, Breton attacked Dostoevsky under the pretext that, writing fiction, he had been forced to utter banalities and to admit impurities into his art. Sartre and his friends detected flaws in Camus' logic, or lack of it, and blamed him for having become one of the French writers most favored by the middle class and, despite his professed unbelief, by the religious souls.[19]

The truth appears to be that a certain weariness with Dostoevsky crept in after 1950 or thereabout in many minds in France and elsewhere. To the young, he then stood as the novelist who had enraptured their fathers in 1920–35, and they were eager to find new idols, which would be their own. He had indeed become a classic, on whom learned essays were being written. His sources were being explored by scholars, who stressed his early affinities with Balzac, George Sand, Schiller. They insisted upon the need to replace him in his historical context, that of the Russian ideology of 1860–80, of the nihilists and the Slavophils, if he were to be understood aright. Indeed, early in his career (in 1861) Dostoevsky himself had submitted that "art is always real and contemporary; it always had been and no other art could exist. . . . the great writer was he who perceived a certain type of man as contemporary."[20] Scholars who were familiar with the Russian language (no French writer of note had been since Mérimée) were able to denounce some distortions in the very personal interpretations of Dostoevsky that had been offered by Gide, Suarès, Faure, and Camus. The admiration of the earlier devotees of Dostoevsky had gone to the saints in his novels—Myshkin or Alyosha. Critics with cooler judgment pointed out that those saints seldom have the last word or the better of the argument in the novels: Ivan is more convincing as a dialectician and more gripping in his inner debates than the characters who are prodigies of humility and forbearance.

As France became convinced, in the second half of the present century, that she had better accept the modern world, with its pursuit of efficiency and of productivity, she also became more critical of certain theses upheld by the former convict turned conservative: that materialism and atheism inevitably lead to socialism and to the enslavement of the individual. Discontent with progress and prosperity will be voiced loudly by the French, louder than in present day Russia. A higher standard of living will not necessarily entail more spiritual quietude. But few, even among the new builders of utopias, are ready to turn their backs upon the benefits that have accrued from a socialist way of life. Dostoevsky's didacticism, so prominent in his novels, could hardly convince his Western readers that there can be no other source of morality than religion. Gide could at one time be fascinated by the famous assertion of Shatov, ready to choose Christ over truth, if he had to make the choice, and if Christ were not *the* Truth. That must be nevertheless a disturbing eventuality to envisage for a believer. The theocentrism of the Russian can appeal only to a minority in a world that many judge to be de-Christianized. Few novelists, even among the most ardent believers, would dare to write Christian works today. The Devil was in vogue for a time, with Gide, Bernanos, Jouhandeau, Julien Green. He provides sinning characters with a convenient alibi. But he also arouses our skepticism. Dostoevsky needed him to confound Ivan Karamazov; his genius was able to impose that outlandish Adversary upon our disbelief. But such legerdemain was also a facile, and not altogether fair, device to which the novelist resorted when he felt powerless to confute Ivan's superb dialectics.

The French are not alone in their eagerness to separate the ethical and religious thinker in Dostoevsky from the novelist. A typical remark from an anonymous English reviewer of new books on Dostoevsky, in the *Times Literary Supplement* of September 20, 1947, ran:

> Dostoevsky's society is a society of screaming people living intolerably on their nerves. Profound flashes of insight come from strange, twisted, schizophrenic souls, but it usually requires the eye of faith and the discernment of charity to see any influence of their faith upon their conduct. . . .

A disenchanted American poet and critic, Kenneth Rexroth, goes further: he contends that the French and the British have grossly overpraised the Russian novelist because they read him in translations that "erased the newspaper-serial vulgarity of his prose style and disguised the formlessness of his narrative."[21] That is claiming a great deal for translations and setting little store by the critical faculties of European admirers of Dostoevsky. To that reader, those novels are not worthy of being called tragedies because characters talk too garrulously "about things that adults learn it is better to be quiet about." They are complicated forces at best, and in *The Brothers Karamazov* the novelist merely mocks us, and mocks himself.

We know too much about Dostoevsky today to romanticize him as the French did for nearly half a century. The subtle humor and the deceptive simplicity of Chekhov have held an appeal for us perhaps more lasting than the inconsistencies and the metaphysical anxieties of Dostoevskian characters. The recent novel in France has renounced any exploration in depth of the psychological contradictions in man and elected to turn against character portrayal and meaningful dialogues calling everything into question. Our contemporaries probably feel inadequate in comparison with the giants of the last century who revolutionized fiction and our view of human nature along with it. After having bowed to the impact of that hurricane from the East, not a few succesors to Gide, Suarès, Proust, and Camus probably would respond today less sarcastically than did Gide to the famous, frightened, and naive announcement by Vogüé in 1886: "Here comes the Scythian, the true Scythian, to revolutionize all our intellectual habits." The revolution has taken place, and its shock has been absorbed. It has enriched the West.

## NOTES

1. A Columbia University thesis by Vladimir Seduro (or Siadura), *Dostoevsky in Russian Literary Criticism, 1846–1956* (Columbia University Press, 1958) summarizes the Russian critics of the novelist. The volume by Mischa Harry Fayer, *Gide, Freedom and Dostoevsky* (Middlebury, Vermont, 1946) fails to keep the promises of its title.

2. Leo Tolstoy, who never liked his great contemporary, declared in a letter to Korolenko, which apparently was not actually sent, that he felt unable to understand why Dostoevsky was so widely read: "For all those Idiots, Adolescents, Raskolinikov and others, that is not the way things happened; it was far easier to understand!" (quoted in Nina Gourfinkel, *Dostoevsky notre contemporain*, Paris: C. Lévy, 1961, p. 100). Maxim Gorky recommended the "far healthier" Pushkin to his compatriots and to foreigners. He attacked Dostoevsky bluntly in an address to the Congress of Soviet Writers, August 17, 1934 (Gorky, *On Literature*, Moscow: Foreign Languages Publishing House, n. d.), and hoped that the influence of Dostoevsky on Western Europe would act like a poison and destroy the psychical balance of the European bourgeois.

3. Already at the end of *L'Immoraliste*, while Michel was, with eagerness and yet with sorrowful love, watching his wife die, he had remarked: "And who will say how many passions and how many thoughts inimical to each other may coexist in man?"

4. Gide became fond of quoting, as one of the mottoes he had adopted,

a line from a late poem by Browning, "A Death in the Desert": "I say that man was made to grow, not stop." In 1938, he celebrated Browning in his journals (March 13) for enabling his reader to envision the glorious possibilities of human nobleness. But, much earlier, while he was preparing his Dostoevsky lectures (*Journals,* Nov. 29, 1921), he was already declaring Browning "a headier beverage" than Dostoevsky. In part, he added, because he only understood Browning's difficult English imperfectly and thus saw him through a mist; he was then practising his English.

A person who observed Gide closely for many years and reported his conversations faithfully, Maria van Rysselberghe, wrote that Gide wanted to admire Dostoevsky, or thought he did; but, in truth, he preferred "the arabesque of *La Princesses de Clèves,* the perfection of the paragraph in Flaubert's prose. Dostoevsky does not have stylized paragraphs, because, in the great momentous scenes, he knows no respite." In July 1919, she asked him: "Which is the novelist that you would have preferred to be? Without hesitation, he answered: Dostoevsky. Ah! He added in a tone of anguish: I fear I am only a theoretician." Elsewhere, he stated how much he envied Dostoevsky for "his gift for inventing events which would show psychological truths." Maria van Rysselberghe, *Les Cahiers de la petite Dame, 1918–29,* Preface by André Malraux (Gallimard, 1973), pp. xxiii and 111.

5. The essay in three parts, "French Letters and the War," is translated by Blanche Price in *The Ideal Reader, Selected Essays by Jacques Rivière* (New York: Meridian Books, 1960), pp. 263-78. In the same volume is found the brief article on "Dostoevsky and the Creation of Character," pp. 245–48, more appositely entitled in French, "De Dostoevsky et de l'insondable," which had appeared in the *Nouvelle Revue française* in February 1922, pp. 175–78.

6. In point of fact, Suarès had been reading Dostoevsky, as well as Tolstoy, whom, like Romain Rolland, his Ecole Normale friend, he preferred, for several years. That has been ably and conclusively shown by Mario Maurin in an article on "The Gide-Suarès Relations," *Yale French Studies,* Gide Issue, No. 7 (1951), pp. 115–24.

7. Besides the two volumes mentioned in the text (*Trois Hommes* and *Présences,* both made up of essays first published elsewhere), André Suarès devoted three burning pages to the exaltation of Dostoevsky in a subsequent book, *Valeurs* (Grasset, 1936), pp. 302–05. Again, he placed the Russian novelist close to Shakespeare and vindicated his strangeness, called madness by some, as a richer and sharper vision than ours. See the article by Sister Madeleine, O S U, "Mauriac and Dostoev-

sky: Psychologists of the Unconscious," in *Renascence,* 5, No. 1 (1952), 7–14.

8. Alain-Fournier and Jacques Rivière, *Correspondance* (Gallimard, 1928), IV, p. 85 (letter of March 3, 1909). The two words "everything explicable" are probably an allusion to an oft-quoted verse in Claudel's *La Ville,* where a person addresses the poet: "O poet, you explain nothing, but all things, through you, become explicable." T. S. Eliot's curious letter to John Pope, published with Eliot's permission in *American Literature* in January 1947 (Vol. 18, No. 4) was brought to my attention by Professor Pope.

9. Strangely, it is in that very same book, *The Idiot,* warmly praised by several French Catholics, that Myshkin, apparently voicing his creator's views, assails Catholicism most bitterly as "an unChristian religion, worse than atheism itself; . . . for it preaches a distorted Christ, . . . the opposite of Christ: the Antichrist."

10. See Melvin Seiden, "Nabokov and Dostoevsky," *Contemporary Literature* (Wisconsin), 13 No. 4 (Autumn 1972), 423–44. The critic finds that, nevertheless, there are some Dostoevskian features to the character of Lolita.

11. A few critics have touched on the subject of Proust's opinion of Dostoevsky and of his hypothetical debt to him, but with prudence: Maurice Bardèche, *Proust romancier* (Les sept Couleurs, 1971), I, p. 331 and II, pp. 245–61; Jean-Yves Tadié, *Proust et le roman* (Gallimard, 1971), pp. 362-63, 408–10; and René de Chantal, *Marcel Proust critique littéraire* (Université de Montréal, 1967), II, pp. 525–30.

12. François Mauriac, *Le Roman* (1928), collected in his *Oeuvres complètes* (Fayard, 1950), VIII, Ch. vi. *Le Romancier et ses personnages* (1933) is reprinted in the same volume. The lines on "The Great Inquisitor" are in *Le nouveau Bloc-Notes, 1958–60* (Flammarion, 1961), pp. 150–52 (Jan. 2 and 5, 1959).

13. The Catholic writer Luc Estang, in his *Présence de Bernanos* (Plon, 1947) is the one who has drawn the analogies between the two novelists most convincingly. He does not, however, conclude that Dostoevsky had any direct influence on Bernanos. Nor does the author of the soundest and fullest volume on Bernanos, Max Milner, in *Bernanos* (Desclée de Brouwer, 1967). Georges Poulet, in a remarkable essay on Bernanos in *Le Point de départ* (Plon, 1964) mentions the inescapable analogy between him and Dostoevsky, but only in passing.

14. Several of the best studies on Malraux have not failed to notice the similarities between his world and that of Dostoevsky. One of the earliest and most fervid in tone was by Rachel Bespaloff, who had spoken

Dostoevsky's own language, in her volume *Cheminements et Carrefours* (Vrin, 1938), pp. 22–58. Wilbur Frohock has penetrating observations on the Dostoevskian aspects of Clappique in his *Malraux and the Tragic Imagination* (Stanford University Press, 1952), pp. 72–75. Denis Boak, one of the few writers on Malraux who stubbornly resists his fascination, touches on the subject in the conclusion of his volume *Malraux* (Oxford: the Clarendon Press, 1968), pp. 205–08. The most precise and the most acute remarks on the analogies between the fictional techniques of the two novelists is found in the study by Jean Carduner, *La Création romanesque chez Malraux* (Nizet, 1968). A parallel sketched between Kirilov and Chen is less convincingly attempted by André Lorant, *Orientations étrangères chez Malraux* (Minard, 1971).

15. In a letter to his American admirer and benefactor, Milton Hindus, Céline expressed a strong distaste for Dostoevsky, "too sinister, too Russian, sickening in his adoration of the convict's jail." *L'Herne*, volume on *Céline*, II, p. 92 (letter of August 23, 1947).

16. The most popular collection of texts on existentialism used in American colleges, by Walter Kaufmann, opens with the *Notes from the Underground* and is entitled *Existentialism from Dostoevsky to Sartre* (New York: Meridian Books, 1956).

17. Albert Camus, "Kirilov," *Le Mythe de Sisyphe* (Pléiade, p. 186).

18. An answer given to Jean-Claude Brisville and reported by Jacques Brenner in the issue of *La Table ronde* devoted to Camus (No. 146, Feb. 1960, p. 99). A small volume has pointed out, and probably magnified, the analogies between *La Chute* and *Notes from the Underground*: Ernest Sturm, *Conscience et Impuissance chez Dostoevsky and Camus* (Nizet, 1967).

19. Breton's vituperations were published in the weekly *Arts*, Oct. 2, 1951. Camus answered, in texts included in the Pléiade edition of his *Essais*, pp. 731–36. The controversy with Sartre and Jeanson was aired in *Les Temps modernes* of May and Aug. 1952. The debate was magnified into "l'affaire de l'Homme révolté."

20. The sentences are quoted in a striking series of articles on "Le Grand Inquisiteur" in *Cahiers du Sud*, Nos. 383–84. (Aug.-Oct. 1965), of which the first, by Charles Corbet, is entitled "Dostoevsky en son temps."

# 2. The Notion of the Absurd in Contemporary French Literature

IN NO COUNTRY PERHAPS, not even Germany, have the bonds between literature and philosophy been closer than in France. French education, which traditionally devotes the last year of secondary school to the almost sole study of philosophy, may account in part for this. The emphasis, through school and college, is on general ideas. There are few French artists and writers who have not felt impelled to extract a philosophy from their novels, poems, and paintings. Science and philosophy have often been practiced by the same men, not only in the century of Descartes and Pascal, but by D'Alembert and Condorcet, Comte, Cournot, Claude Bernard, Henri Poincaré. Stendhal's novels cannot be fully understood without some account of the psychology of Condillac, Balzac's without Swedenborg, Zola and the naturalists without some knowledge of Taine's ideas, Anatole France without Renan, much of symbolism without Bergsonism.

Never has that permeation of literature with philosophy been more marked than around and since World War II. Translations of Hegel and commentaries on his work suddenly blossomed then; Nietzsche was revaluated and proved as dynamic an influence as Marx. Existentialism provided the background and the ideology for much of the literature of the years 1940-60. Books, especially by Englishmen, were written on the novelists and dramatists of that era under such titles as *Literature Considered as Philosophy* (by Everett Knight, 1957), *The Novelist as Thinker* (B. Rajan, ed., 1947), *The Novelist as Philosopher* (John Cruickshank, ed., 1962). Struc-

57

turalism, which attempted to replace existentialism as the philosophy
of the 1960's, has produced an equally imposing mass of creative and
critical literature, much of it, no doubt, of an ephemeral character.

Among the developments, affecting both the realm of ideas and
that of imaginative creation, is one that is among the least understood
in this country and indeed one of the most surprising to occur in a
land that traditionally has passed for the home of logic and of cold
rationalism; that is, the fascination with the absurd among many a
thinker, dramatist, and novelist of France.

The word "absurd" naturally is not new, although it does not
appear to have had an equivalent in the Greek language. It first
occurs in one of the philosophical treatises of Cicero. But the word
"logic" was likewise not used by the greatest logician of all times,
Aristotle. The process of a *reductio ad absurdum* existed, whether
or not the word "absurd" was used, as in the famous paradoxes of
Zeno of Elea, which proved the impossibility of motion. The concept
of absurdity, somewhat different from "unreason" and from "non-
sense" (a word that has regrettably degenerated in English), obviously occurred to some of the earliest speculators on epistemology.

The novelty, however, is that a whole era, around the middle of
the present century, has boasted of being the era of the absurd; on
its dialectics of absurdity, its pride in having plumbed the depths of
the absurd, it has erected a literature, an ethics, a philosophy leading
to action and even to optimism.

The French have never quite admitted, despite the many foreigners
who have dubbed them "Cartesian" and "enamored with logic," that
they are a nation of rationalists, even less a reasonable people. A
number of their thinkers have derided the claims of reason and, with
Pascal, even with Montaigne, but less passionately with him, preferred the leap of faith. With conviction, like Pascal, with subtlety
and perhaps with some perfidy, like Montaigne, they have submitted
that the ultimate move of reason is to acknowledge that many things
transcend it, or lie beyond its reach. Rousseau is not alone in his century, commonly taken to be an age of reason, to have challenged the
analytical thinking processes of his contemporaries and to have
advocated a humbler but higher wisdom. Wordsworth does not
hesitate to assert, in Rousseauistic fashion, in "The Tables Turned":

> One impulse from a vernal wood
> May teach you more of man,
> Of moral evil and of good
> Than all the sages can.

Étienne Gilson remarked, in an article on the death of Bergson, that if France did not periodically produce those thinkers who question or circumscribe the role of reason there would be far fewer Frenchmen deserving to be called intelligent. But neither among the illuminists and the mystics of the eighteenth century nor even among the Dadaists and their followers, the surrealists, had there been so many serious authors as there are now joyfully wallowing in the absence of any logical or rational significance. The new romantics of our day exult in the privilege of that tragic anguish which they take to be their private blessing. That proclamation of universal absurdity is looked upon by many of them as a new *tabula rasa,* upon which they may attempt to build up firmer foundations for the future.

The curious feature of this passion for absurdity (for, with one of those writers, Camus, it is nothing less than a passion) is that it was not in the aftermath of the First or of the Second World War that it asserted itself, but, like much that is significant today, at the end of the first decade of the twentieth century and that it should have flourished most robustly in France, at one and the same time the most conservative and the most revolutionary of countries, and allegedly the altar of the cult of reason.

The word "reason" in English and in the Romance languages originated from the past participle *"ratus"* of the verb *"reri"* by way of the intermediary substantive *"ratio."* The verb connoted the meaning of "counting," "reckoning," hence accounting through what preceded and was perhaps a cause of what followed. Science, philosophy, criticism may be prophecy and project themselves forward, as the existentialists are fond of claiming; those forms of knowledge may even hope to work upon the future and to forestall what appears ominous in it. But they first must take stock of what is, in the present, and resort to the past in order to disentangle the forces that have molded the present. In that sense, Kierkegaard's epigrammatic remark, reported by his countryman Harald Höffding, is incisively just: "We live forward, but we understand backward."

Then, especially with Descartes, the connotations linked with the word *"ratio"* or "reason" became enlarged through the accretion of some at least of the meanings attached to the Greek substantive *"Logos."* The French language, like the English, has chosen to use *"le Verbe"* or "the Word" to render the meaning of *"Logos"* as used in neo-Platonic philosophy and in the first verse of the fourth Gospel; there lies more mystery in *"le Verbe,"* viewed as an hypostasis or emanation of God, than in the all too human term *"raison."* Descartes, without ever defining the word "reason" very precisely, severed it from authority, from the tradition embodied in the Church and, generally speaking, from memory. He endowed reason with an overruling faculty in man that evolves principles from which deductions will ensue and that aims at organizing the universe. It places essence as anterior and superior to existence and proceeds from thought to existence. Reason provides a necessary order that extends from thought to things; it creates frameworks or "cadres" within which we lodge our experience. Spinoza represents one of the summits of rationalism when he proclaims that it is in the nature of reason to consider things not as contingent but as necessary. In the fourth book of his *Ethics,* he gravely and grandiosely asserts: "There is given in nature no singular thing more useful to mankind than a man living under the conduct of Reason." Leibniz exalts into a fundamental principle, *principium magnum, grande et nobilissimum,* the assertion that *nihil est sine ratione,* "nothing is without reason," the word reason being more all-embracing than "cause."

It has been maintained, and on firm evidence, that the greatest influence of Descartes' rationalism (but not of his scientific theories) was felt, not by his French contemporaries and immediate followers, but by the eighteenth century. Certain it is that the doctrine of indefinite and even necessary progress, resting upon the spread of reason, gained favor in the Age of Enlightenment, from Fontenelle to Condorcet. Since reason was the most widely spread of man's "faculties" or privileges and since the French way of conceiving reason was taken to be the model for all others and universal, the self-assigned task of thinking men was to enlighten others and to spread the realm of reason through education and through freeing one's fellow beings from superstition and from the sway of priests. The more we know, the more power we acquire to improve men and institutions, and presumably the better we act. The literature of knowledge and the literature of power, as De Quincey was to call them, would be united.

Much of the literature of the nineteenth century—even when, with the romantics, it railed against a universe deaf to human complaints and especially when it described reality with some elaborateness—rested implicitly upon the notion that there is a pattern inherent in the world, that, as Hegel put it, the real is rational. The other half of the Hegelian formula was accepted by a number of philosophers (though not by Hegel's stubborn derider and foe, Schopenhauer): the rational is real, and history unfolds as the reign of reason extending over the world; reason is the working of a God in becoming, and the kingdom of God is reached through man. If the world is not comprehensible and if philosophers have vainly attempted to understand it as a follower of Hegel become his critic, Karl Marx, was to assert, man's task is to change it. But there was little attempt to deny the possibility of an almost self-evident correspondence between the mind of man—that microcosm—and the macrocosm of the universe.

A series of denials of such a reassuring conformity between man and the world, and of vehement rejections of logic as a guarantee of accurate reasoning, was loudly formulated early in the twentieth century by a growing number of French authors. Many of them had been touched, twenty or twenty-five years after he stopped writing, by Nietzsche's assaults on rationalism as adopted by German metaphysicians. It has, for over a century, been the role of poets and artists to spurn analytical dissection and prosaic common sense. A sentence of Rimbaud's *Season in Hell* began to be adopted as a slogan by the French students rebelling against the worship of clarity and order: "I ended by finding sacred the disorder of my mind." Gide's *Fruits of the Earth,* published in 1897, took more than a dozen years to reach, at last, a public. "Ah! who will liberate my mind from the heavy fetters of logic?," he had called in one of the litanies of that volume of poetic prose. In 1907, in his *Creative Evolution,* the philosopher Bergson, in his smooth, calm, un-Nietzschean way, quietly submitted that "intelligence is characterized by a natural inability to understand life." That had been the implicit message of many a symbolist poet, between 1885 and 1900, drawn to some form of mysticism or to occultism.

At the same time or a little later, just before the outbreak of World War I, more and more scientists, anticipating some of the interpretations of relativity and even the principle of indeterminacy, questioned whether science does grasp and explain reality itself or merely evolves a provisionally coherent body of notions relative to things and parallel to them. The appearance of Freudian psycho-analysis dealt a blow to the champions of reason, and even to the clear-sightedness long dear to the French, for it seemed that our fully conscious life and the exercise of our intellect stood at the mercy of dreams, urges, desires, over which our reason seldom held sway. Cultured men and timorous bourgeois were scandalized, in Vienna as in Paris. Hardly were they getting accustomed to some of the Freudian views than a dissenter from Freudianism, C. G. Jung, offered the no less brutal contention that many of our thoughts, impulses, and actions are controlled by ancestral forces, archetypes, and age-old myths, the symbolism of which might be unravelled; but their power over us would hardly fall within the ever-shrinking kingdom of reason. Realism and naturalism in fiction were discarded by the compatriots of Proust, Giraudoux, and Cocteau as well as by those of Virginia Woolf and of D. H. Lawrence. The principles of identity or of noncontradiction were flouted by dramatists and novel-ists who revelled in an altogether free and capricious fantasy. The supernatural invaded many short stories. Coherency in characters and consistency of behavior were thrown to the winds.

World War I, once the short-lived flush of patriotic enthusiasm had vanished, appeared to many participants and observers as the shattering of all reasonableness and the fierce trampling underfoot of all hopes once aroused by the spread of rationalism. French and British democracies could demand from their citizens in arms what kings and emperors had seldom dared ask from them: incredible ordeals in filth and gore to capture a few yards of trenches at Verdun or half an acre of mud in Flanders. Still, people attempted to make some sense out of it all, through lofty slogans about establishing security and just peace for the ages; others clung to the notion that their absurd plight throughout that insensate mass slaughter had been due to a plot of greedy munitions makers and that universal socialism alone, curbing voracious and ruthless capitalism, could restore a rational and generous order to Europe. The hope was nurtured of some other form of society, in the East or in Communist Russia, that might promise less absurdity and more emotional solace to a war-ridden continent. Young men and women, utopian intellectuals, disheartened by the vagaries of capitalism after 1929 and by the stupidity of millions of unemployed while coal, meat, cotton, coffee could not be sold and the surplus of goods was destroyed, looked up to "that great light in the East," the torch lit in Moscow or the nonviolence of Gandhi.

The Moscow trials, the dictatorship of Stalin crushing all dissenters, the ascent of Hitler rallying thousands of German professors, writers, scientists, pastors around him, the self-deception of the Western democracies refusing to concede the obvious, then the outbreak of another world war and, in France, the collapse of the ruling, and presumably intelligent, classes in 1940, all that reinforced the conviction that absurdity was ruling unchallenged in Europe. In the nations that had hitherto passed for the most advanced and the most progressive in science, education, and philosophy, the daily press had become infested with vapid propaganda; the mass media had been taken over by peddlers of blatant insults and of lies that should have revolted the critical spirit of the people. The memory of those years 1930–40, perhaps the most shameful in the history of Western Europe, was long to rankle in those who then decided to come out of the isolation in which writers of earlier eras had chosen to seclude themselves. In France, Malraux, Sartre, Anouilh, Ionesco, Genet, Camus, Beckett, and many a figure of lesser magnitude were, in varying manners, compelled to come to grips with the problem of the absurd.

The theme became most prominent in the plays that captured the public's attention around 1950; that implied a total reversal of what had been the course of the French theater since the classical age. A book by Martin Esslin, *The Theatre of the Absurd* (1961), and several controversies among reviewers and irate or amused playgoers have drawn our attention to this undertaking, which aimed at nothing less than a systematic wrecking of all that had constituted the fabric of the traditional theater. The playwright refuses, in that absurdist theater, to delineate characters and to offer a consistent portrait of individuals. He renounces consistency, the accumulative effects of a progression from act to act, all logical and rational devices. Heroes disappear, and characters no longer are punished or rewarded with a clearer insight into themselves, like Oedipus, or perhaps Lear, for some tragic flaw. They are not the architects of their fate. The audience is not presented with the reassuring picture of a coherent individual, still less with one who analyzes himself relentlessly as in Racine or Marivaux. It is not favored with the possibility of assuming the superior and condescending attitude of an onlooker watching puppets tossed about by fate. The characters of Ionesco, Beckett, Adamov, or Arrabal stubbornly refuse to have any meaning. "We are not beginning to . . . mean something, are we?" questions Ham, aghast at such a dreaded possibility, in Beckett's *Endgame*. Language is denounced by these dramatists of the absurd as a mere string of silly trivialities and clichés, irrational and inane. A character named Nicholas, in Ionesco's *Victims of Duty* (1953), serves as the mouthpiece of the author, who fifteen years later, was to be elected to the once traditional fortress of conventional logic, the French Academy:

> I dream of an irrationalist theatre. . . . Today's theatre is not attuned to the cultural style of our age. . . . Drawing my inspiration from another logic and another psychology, I would like to bring contradiction into the noncontradiction in what common sense deems to be contradictory. . . . We shall renounce the principle of identity and of the unity of characters, to the advantage of motion, of a dynamic psychology. . . . Personality does not exist. There are only in ourselves contradictory or noncontradictory forces.

The French existentialists have been rather chary of acknowledging any debt to their predecessors among their own countrymen. True it is that the philosophy of the absurd had not been formulated by the French thinkers of the nineteenth century, not even by those who disbelieved in reason. But in 1926 a young author of twenty-five, then almost unknown, André Malraux, had published an imaginary correspondence between a Westerner and a Chinese. The latter, reflecting on the strange ways of loving, of worshipping, of facing death that he had observed in France, concluded: "At the center of the European man, there lurks an essential absurdity which controls all the moves of existence." His French correspondent, who writes very much like Malraux himself, fails to deny such an assertion. He agrees in a tragic tone: "The absurd, the lovely absurd, linked to us like the serpent to the tree of Good and Evil, is never quite hidden, and we see him preparing its most alluring wiles with the devoted assistance of our own will." From that ubiquitous absurdity, however, Malraux attempted to escape, through action, through fraternity with other dwellers in that absurd world, through laying a new groundwork for the erection of an imposing monument to the permanence of cultures and to the unity of mankind: art was to provide that foundation for an eventual salvaging of our heritage.

Two years before that early work of Malraux appeared, in which few critics then discerned the promise of a great writer, there had died, in the midst of even darker obscurity, Franz Kafka. He was to be much read in France in the late thirties, at the very time when, as a Jew, he was posthumously ignored in Nazi Germany. Camus, Sartre, Gide himself were deeply impressed by him. But the absurdity that strikes us in Kafka's universe is very different from that which Camus would place at the core of his philosophical meditation. Kafka is an alienated man, as a man among women with whom he hesitates to associate lastingly, as a Jew in Austria-Hungary, as a Czech who writes in the German language, as a man doomed to sickness in a world at war. Not only Ionesco, Beckett, Adamov, Arrabal, but Camus himself similarly became alienated men, able to see the French language and French culture both from the inside and with detachment. Camus, moreover, felt severed from the world of fighting men or of athletes by a disease similar to Kafka's, tuberculosis. But the Czech novelist never asserted the absurd meaninglessness of the universe. To Joseph K. and other impersonations of the author, there is a meaning somewhere in the universe. But that universe baffles them. They strive arduously to understand, to bow to laws and conventions meekly, to conform, and to unravel the enigma. But the order of the world is inhuman and undecipherable. They consent to their own doom and accept the harsh verdict that condemns them.

The *locus classicus* among the few Sartrian depictions of the intrusion of the absurd into an all too placid and stagnating existence occurs in Sartre's masterpiece in comic and philosophical fiction, *Nausea.* Roquentin, after his mournful wanderings in the city of Bouville and his dull musings in the public library, has just had an illumination, a caricature of an epiphany, in the public garden. He observed a black, knotty root of a chestnut tree, and he suddenly was visited by the revelation of existence. That root existed; and the lawn, the bench, a statue amid a copse of bushes, they all existed. They existed in an obscene nudity. There was a proliferation of matter there, indifferent to man. All objects, and the man watching them, were *de trop*—one, or several, too many. There could be no other relationship among them but that of mutual superfluousness. His life, his eventual death, were all unneeded, *de trop.* "I was *de trop* for eternity," concluded Roquentin. And the word "absurdity" forces its way into his novel-diary. "Absurdity: it was not an idea in my head, or a whisper, but that long dead serpent at my feet, that wooden serpent." The awesome discovery made by the diarist is that of his own contingency. All is contingent, gratuitous, superfluous. It might very well not have been. The absurdity of it all overwhelms Roquentin with nausea. From there he starts again and attempts to give significance to what has had none.

In a little-known interview given to Christian Grisoli and reported in *Paru* (Dec. 1945), Sartre clearly outlined one of the several points of difference between Camus and himself:

> Camus' philosophy is a philosophy of the absurd; for him, the absurd springs from the relation between man and the world, from man's reasonable demands and the irrationality of the world. . . . In my eyes there is no such abrurdity, in the sense of scandal or of deception. What I call absurd is very different. It is the universal contingency of the being which is, but which is not the foundation of its being; it is what in the being is given, unjustifiable, always primary.

The true optimist in that sense is Sartre rather than Camus; for Sartre asserts the freedom of the thing for itself, that which is not what it is and is what it is not, since it constantly projects itself forward. Our own choice is autonomous. We create our own values and invest our past with a meaning. In a curious footnote to *Being and Nothingness* (III, iii, 3), Sartre indeed does not exclude the possibility of an ethics of salvation and deliverance. Camus is more stubbornly anti-Christian and indicts hope as the worst subterfuge offered by religion to keep us from intoxicating ourselves with the absurd and from revolting.

Sartre was generous in the remark quoted above, uttered while he was assisting Camus in establishing himself with the French public; he termed Camus "a philosopher of the absurd." But he added that, despite his frequent mention of Kierkegaard, Kafka, and Nietzsche, Camus really stood in the tradition of the seventeenth-century French moralists. Camus himself had proudly asserted such an affinity in an important essay in *Confluences* (Lyon, 1943), *Problèmes du roman*. He had praised there the "passionate monotony" of classical masterpieces and ventured the assertion that "to be classical means to repeat oneself and to know how to repeat oneself." Taken literally, such a quality was possessed preeminently by Hugo or Péguy at their most repetitious moments. But *The Myth of Sisyphus,* which Camus brought out in 1942, does stand among the most obsessively repetitious books, averse to the conciseness and to the clarity of the allegedly Cartesian nation. It is no more linear and rigidly systematic as a philosophy than most books by Kierkegaard or by Nietzsche. But it is all the more moving, and it has proved all the more influential for it.

Camus nowhere defines the word "absurd" unambiguously. But the student of the classics that he had been was aware of the etymological meaning of the adjective in which *"ab"* serves as intensive prefix to the adjective *"surdum"* (in the accusative), which has given *"sourd"* in French and *"sordo"* in Italian and Spanish. Its meaning was "discordant," what grates on our ears and would make us deaf, what is jarring. *"Absurde canere"* was in Latin "to sing out of tune." Such discordance was soon extended to what strikes us as unreasonable in an assertion, to what is so impossible as to be dismissed outright. In mathematics and logics, a *reductio ad absurdum* is a way of refuting a patently impossible proposition. But the word "absurd" acquired its letters of nobility when some Christian apologists explained that one of the most powerful arguments for faith lay precisely in claiming its very absurdity. "Credo quia absurdum" is a phrase that is commonly taken (and hardly legitimately) to sum up Pascal's apologetic conclusion. In fact, a North African Father of the Church, Tertullian, wrote in his treatise *De Carne Christi,* Chapter v, that Christ did rise from the dead; it appears impossible to our understanding, but that is precisely why it must be believed. "Credibile est, quia ineptum est; et sepultus resurrexit; certum est, quia impossibile." That countryman of Saint Augustine, whom he preceded by two hundred years, and of Camus is a turbid but passionately energetic thinker, throwing many a challenge to timid logic. Camus likewise declared: "It is absurd that it should be thus, but it is thus." He accepted that absurdity, looked at it straightforwardly, and started from there to attempt a reconstruction of his mental and spiritual fabric. "To acknowledge the absurdity of life cannot be an end, but merely a beginning," Camus stated in 1939 in *Alger républicain* in a commentary on Sartre's short story "Le Mur."

Camus denounced the dissonance that led him to feel not *de trop,* but cloven in two in this absurd world. Man wishes to be immortal, or to believe that something of himself may survive, and he is confronted at every step with the omnipresence of death. He yearns for justice, but, ever since Job's lamentations on the unintelligible workings of a supreme Being who rewards the wicked and chastises the just, he has found injustice deriding his faith. The sight of Germany triumphant in 1940–42 (when *The Myth of Sisyphus* was being written) and the prudent silence of the voices of spiritual powers that should have clamored for justice naturally left a deep scar on Camus' generation. Never did he write more vibrant prose than in his *Letters to a German Friend.* Man also cries out his need for an intelligible order in the universe, but he soon has to concede that the real is hardly rational and that the order of thought and the order of things do not necessarily fit. Man desperately searches for clarity, if not as a ready-made transparence that makes everything too easy, at least as a goal to be reached by the inquisitive mind after it emerges from darkness or murkiness. There again he is baffled. "Nothing is clear, all is chaos, and man retains only his own clearsightedness and the precise knowledge of the walls imprisoning him. . . . What is absurd is the confrontation between that irrationality [of the world] and that wild desire for clarity, the call of which resounds in the deepest in man."

Other writers, similarly athirst for a presence in or outside the universe to watch benevolently over them, or at the very least to heed their prayers, chose to pour out their complaints to God or, like Alfred de Vigny, to punish the Deity by haughtily refusing to believe in Him. Or, like Baudelaire, they preferred a mordant Satanism and sneered bitterly at the order of things amid which they felt unattuned and discordant. Baudelaire, in the poem in which he most savagely flagellates himself, declared:

> Ne suis-je pas un faux accord
> Dans la divine symphonie,
> Grâce à la vorace Ironie
> Qui me secoue et qui me mord ?

("Am I not a faulty chord in the divine symphony, thanks to the voracious Irony which shakes and stings me in torment?") Camus is no less a romantic than those poets, and he too spurns the gods, but with no declamation and with no anger. Sisyphus becomes his symbolic hero. Alfred de Musset had entertained the project of writing on that mythical king of Corinth or of identifying himself with him. The information bequeathed on Sisyphus by mythographers or ancient poets is too scant for the moderns to have magnified him into an archrebel like Prometheus. Homer has only a passing allusion to him in the sixth canto of the *Iliad* (1. 153) and an eight-line passage in the eleventh canto of the *Odyssey* (ll. 593–600). Ulysses, visiting Achilles, Hercules, and other illustrious dead in Inferno, catches sight of Sisyphus, rolling his stone uphill, exhausted and sweating; not a word of pity, however, is uttered, and no explanation is offered for the crime of the unhappy king who had been sentenced to such a punishment without end.

The peculiarity of Camus' "absurdism" is that it is repeatedly deducted from the author's unbelief or from what Malraux, for whom he entertained a warm admiration, called the end of all absolutes in today's world. While Malraux appeared at times to lament that impossibility of the moderns to accept Christianity or even to live in it as mankind did in earlier centuries "like fish in an aquarium," Camus proudly and flatly refuses to harbor any nostalgia for the lost faith. "Human life," he declares in *The Myth of Sisyphus,* "is a perfect absurdity for him who does not have any faith in immortality." That absurdity imprisons man in a dilemma: either escape from the absurdity through suicide, "the one truly serious philosophical problem," or through hope. But that hope will be neither that which the Christians had long offered as a solace to the dwellers in this vale of tears nor that of the Marxists, ready to open concentration camps and to sentence men to ignoble trials and caricatures of justice in order that a brighter day might dawn for the proletariat at some remote time. To such hope, which he brands as an outright evil because it fosters the placid acceptance of present injustice, Camus prefers revolt. He repeatedly declared that he was no philosopher, and he is not indeed, if to be a philosopher means dealing in abstractions and erecting a comprehensive system in which everything is explained, or explained away. With Kierkegaard and with the phenomenologists, Camus chooses to place existence before thought and to understand the abstract through describing it in concrete terms. Lust for life and for happiness, despite disease and painful polemics, remained primary in Camus. From the phenomenological philosophy, or what of it had reached France by 1942, he had retained the urge to learn anew how to see, how to be attentive, and how to direct one's consciousness toward objects. He expected no solution to the eternal philosophical enigmas. "The doctrines which explain everything to me also weaken me. They unburden me from the weight of my own life; and yet it is up to me, all alone, to bear it." The last words of *The Myth of Sisyphus* invite us to imagine the stoic and proud hero as happy. One is reminded of the Greek god who, in Keats's *Hyperion,* proclaims it the "top of sovereignty" to accept events calmly and to look at truths with unflinching clarity. Oceanus pronounces, in one of the noblest passages in English romantic poetry:

> . . . for to bear all naked truths,
> And to envisage circumstance, all calm,
> That is the top of sovereignty.

Such a stress on the greatness of absurdity as the primary mover in man's endeavor to do away with absolutes and to become, as the modest and compassionate hero of *The Plague* wishes to be, a "saint without God" is part of a general struggle, among French unbelievers and atheists, to appropriate the tragic sense of life once found in Pascal and missing in Voltaire. It does not hint at any envy of those who have found peace of mind and security in their faith; nor does it resemble in any way anticlericalism or Voltairian sarcasms. Camus' writings as a moralist and a journalist teem with reassertions of his stubborn denial of another life after death and of any Christian interpretation of his works, be they *The Plague* ("the most anti-Christian of my books," he called it in 1947 in *Le Monde* ) or *The Fall* (in a statement of August 30, 1956). He was still almost unknown to the general public when, in April 1943, he gave to the *Cahiers du Sud* a revealing article on a book by a French Catholic, Jean Guitton, portraying the touching figure of an ecclesiastic, Monsieur Pouget. That priest, in his tolerant and learned comments on the Scriptures, anticipated Teilhard de Chardin and several Catholic ministers who, in the years 1950 and after, have practically given up miracles, the Revelation, and the stress on the literal truth of every chapter and verse of the Bible. In a footnote to his article, Camus offered this suggestive remark:

> Contemporary unbelief [the French word *"incredulité"* has connotations different from those of *"incroyance"*] no longer rests on science, as it did at the end of the last century. It denies science and religion at one and the same time. It no longer is the skepticism of reason vis à vis the miracle. It is a passionate unbelief.

The last two words aptly express the passionate, ardent, and almost joyful mood in which Camus and other modern French have hailed the philosophical attitude of absurdism. "Absurdity is a passion, the most heart-rending of all passions," Camus confides to his reader in the early chapters of *The Myth of Sisyphus*. Through coming to grips with that notion, or rather with that experience, a thoughtful man is able to propose a saner scale of values in this insane world, rehabilitating the life of the body and of feelings, as well as the virtue of action aimed at assisting others, and answering in the affirmative Nietzsche's disturbing question: "Is ennobling possible?" Radiantly, Camus looks forward to that recuperation by man of his lost kingdom and concludes: "Man again will recover the wine of absurdity and the bread of indifference which nourish his greatness." Through that preliminary ascesis in the stern domain of the absurd, having shaken off the conventional lip service tribute to reason and rationalism, the absurd man may find himself in a favored position to face what is called, in a remark in Camus' posthumous *Notebooks,* "the sole contemporary problem: can one transform the world without believing in the power of reason?"

More and more of Camus' reflections, from *The Myth of Sisyhus* to his Nobel Prize acceptance address in 1958, revolved around the meaning and the place of literature and the arts in this absurd world. The words he uttered and wrote on that subject in his Stockholm address—and prior to that in "Défense de l'intelligence" (March 15, 1954) and "Le Témoin de la liberté" (Nov. 1948)— count among the most cogent apologies for the noble role of the artist in a war-ridden age addicted to ideological hatreds. It is one of the themes recurring in *The Fall*. Already, however, in that handbook for the absurd man entitled *The Myth of Sisyphus,* Camus had questioned himself on the value of his pursuit and calling, that of a man of letters, in a world harassed by immediate economic and moral ills. Like Sartre, he had spurned the facile and vainglorious appeal to posterity and the sacrificing of the present to a "monument more lasting than brass" dreamt of by Horace and Théophile Gautier. "The true generosity toward the future consists in giving everything to the present" is one of the maxims of that moralist in *The Rebel*. Having proclaimed life absurd and having drunk from that assertion an intoxicating draught of courage, the creator does not take refuge in silence, in idle complaint, or in acceptance of what is and in chiselling his own statue or his sentences, like the half-crazy man in *The Plague.*

Camus prefers to resort to the solace exalted in a famous aphorism of Nietzsche, which he quotes: "Art, and nothing but art; we have art in order not to die from truth." Literature and art defend the rights of dialogue, hence of tolerance, in a world all too prone to hate. They afford an absurd joy, which is also, under its appearance of ironical bitterness, an exalting one. "Ironical philosophies are those which make for passionate works." On the shambles of timid logic and of bankrupt rationalism, art arises triumphant. "The work of art stems from the renouncement of the intellect to reasoning in the presence of the concrete. . . . If the world were clear, art would not exist."

This essay on "The notion of the absurd" was written for *Prose,* a biannual magazine published in New York, at 6 St. Luke's Place. It appeared in No. 4, Spring 1972. The publisher, Mr. Coburn Britton, is thanked here for permission to reprint.

# 3. Literature
## and Revolution

Karl Marx is often quoted as having declared that "revolutions are the locomotives of history." Almost any Frenchman, even if he carefully keeps his money in his pocket on the right side, not too far from his liver, which constantly threatens to ache in people of his race afflicted with the Prometheus complex, tucked prudently away from the impulses of his heart, is proud of the many and resonant "locomotives" of which his country's history can boast. One of the most eloquent Frenchmen alive, André Malraux, who enjoyed De Gaulle's confidence and friendship and incurred the violent hatred of the Communists, long was honored for having put in the mouth of one of his characters in *Les Conquérants* (1928) the famous cry: "Revolution . . . all that is not revolution is worse." To him, a disabused revolutionary, she (for the word in French, happily, is feminine) was like the mistress of the torn Latin poet who abjectly confessed to her: "Nec tecum, nec sine te vivere possum."

There ran a thrill of almost erotic joy through many Parisians, young and not so young, when in May 1968 they believed they found themselves in the midst of a revolution and not just a mere riot. For several years their sense of national pride had been humiliated by watching the privilege of launching a revolution ravished from their country, once the nursing home and the model for that sublime process of changing history, and appropriated by arrogant and envious upstarts, in Castro's Cuba, in Mao's China, in Bolivia, at Berkeley, and at Columbia. That particular French revolution soon

74

proved abortive. When the sacrosanct symbols of the consumer society, the automobiles, started being set on fire by the young rioters around the Sorbonne, the French middle class rallied to law and order far more meekly than Americans were to do after the alliterative admonitions of the American Demosthenes, Mr. Agnew; they elected the most conservative government in their recent history.

It may be that France, and even Western Europe, has lost its singularity as the ideal breeding ground of revolutions and that the New World, first South and Central America and now the United States, is to inherit the prerogative of being the revolutionary land. Let us concede that this new image of the United States in the world at large has greatly enhanced the prestige of the American republic. Its history, its philosophy, its art used to be treated contemptuously and condescendingly by the journalists, the intellectuals, the grave bearded sages, and even the teenagers of Europe and Asia. It was granted some achievement in the realm of "know how," but little prestige in the more exalted sphere of "think how."

Suddenly, the whole world started exhibiting American art, imitating American novels, quoting American poetry; the most patronizing of the London literary weeklies admitted that the American imagination had surpassed that of Britain in forcefulness and originality. Continental Europeans and South Americans discovered that the land of business was not necessarily a cultural desert; indeed that more than once, if the business of America could once have been said to be business, art had also become the affair of business firms, and not necessarily for mercantile purposes. Lewis Mumford, one of the most determined crusaders for a finer quality of life in America, remarks at the beginning of his volume *Art and Technics* that "when a Chinese scholar wished to utter a withering curse upon his enemy, he said, 'May you live in an interesting age!' " one, that is, translated in Western terms, "of moral landslides and political earthquakes." We should probably congratulate ourselves for living in such an interesting era.

The word "revolution" implies, ironically, not only an orderly movement in the stars and planets, but that eventually heavenly bodies return to their previous position and the change effected therefore has proved somewhat illusory. Applied to human affairs, often not very rigorously, the word has usually designated the overthrow by force of a government or a legal seizure of power (such as the Nazi party achieved in Germany in 1932–33) by a group that then shakes itself free from all parliamentary restraints and makes havoc of democratic safeguards. A revolution that remained solely on the political plane, however, would not be glorified by the halo that today, in several languages, raises a mystique around the word.

In many a so-called "Latin" country, the legal or the illegal (but soon legalized) overthrow of a ministry or a government amounts to hardly more than the reshuffling of a parliamentary cabinet, as is frequently practiced in nonrevolutionary Britain. A genuine revolution also effects a redistribution of the means of production and of property and, often enough though not necessarily, a brutal change in the daily lives of many and the sacrifice of lives. For many years, such a cataclysm was deemed to be profoundly repugnant to Anglo-Saxon minds. De Tocqueville noted, in the second part of his *Democracy in America*,[1] that "in America, men have the opinions and passions of democracy; in Europe, we have still the passions and opinions of revolution."

Thoughtful historians and political scientists have analyzed not only the concept of revolution but also its multifarious and often imponderable consequences. They have remarked that few such momentous and brutal series of events were ever forecast by the thinkers who were retrospectively singled out as the architects of those changes, be they Montesquieu, Voltaire, Rousseau (who, if they had lived beyond 1793, would probably have perished under the guillotine), Marx or Plekhanov, or the Western observers of China before 1911 or before 1927. They have also warned would-be revolutionaries that in no case, certainly in the twentieth century, has a revolution been followed by a more liberal regime than the one that was overthrown.

Any revolution, even when started and at first led by idealists of good will, finds itself constrained to defend its achievement both against the counterrevolutionary factions intent upon wrecking it and against the extreme left, which refuses to let the revolution be put to an end at a certain time and to establish order. The result has most often been a postrevolutionary government vested in one single party or headed by a dictator, having to install a secret police, and an army much stronger than the one that was overthrown.

Yet an unheard-of vigor accrues to the countries that have effected a revolution, even a bloody one. France after her Terror and her revolutionary wars, Russia twenty-five years after 1917, China under Mao, even Germany after the slaughter of millions of her citizens on the battlefield and in the bombed cities and the even more horrendous disappearance of her Jewish citizens seem to have enjoyed an extraordinary prosperity and reconstituted their science. New layers of the population are tapped by the revolutionary regime; new incentives are offered to citizens no longer hampered by the hierarchies and the privileges of the previous ruling classes; new ideas are tried. Since human life is held in scant regard by the revolutionary rulers, room is forcibly made for the underprivileged of yesterday, promoted overnight to the role of a new and more plebeian elite.

The precedent of the "great" French Revolution is directly relevant to the primary question addressed in this essay: First, because the position then occupied by France in the Western world was not dissimilar from the one that the United States holds today, as the cynosure of all the eyes of the progressive elements in Europe and the country wielding the utmost cultural prestige. Second, because that revolution clearly started in the minds of men and was not due primarily to economic causes, to poverty, or to starvation. Indeed, as Marxist historian Jean Jaurès was the first to proclaim and as one of the latest historians of the French economy in the eighteenth century put it, it came at a time of great economic expansion and was "a Revolution of prosperity."[2]

Literature and ideas played a large part in preparing it. Partly for that reason, and because an extraordinary influence of its principles abroad followed it, magnified, rendered dynamic by literary works of conspicuous merit, that Revolution has proved the most momentous event in world history since the establishment of Christianity. It influenced a dozen attempts at revolution in other countries; it served as a revered model for the South American revolu-

78 LITERATURE AND REVOLUTION

tions, for that of Russia in 1917, and for that of Mao Tse-tung.
"What has been happening in China," wrote the London *Economist*
in February 1967, "is the end of the road that started in Paris in
1789." Compared with it, the English Revolution of 1688 was so
restrained as to have been no revolution at all. The American Revolution (which was for the French an admired precedent and a
model), probably because it has not been presented dynamically in
literature of the highest order, has exerted no influence on the
European and South American revolutions of the nineteenth century
or on those of Africa and Asia in our own time.

The late Harvard historian Crane Brinton devoted a volume to
*The Anatomy of Revolutions* (1938).[3] He selected four instances
of revolutionary upheavals: England in 1688, the American Revolution, the French, the Russian. All of them occurred in societies
that were economically progressive and not at all during a period
of acute depression. But all of them had been preceded, and probably
prepared by, wide disaffection from the regime and from its lack of
glamor, one might say, of poetry, on the part of the intellectual
elites. That disaffection was fostered by literature that, imaginatively
and intellectually, had indicted the prevailing state of affairs and
the selfish obtuseness of the ruling class and offered a glimpse of a
drastic change through which more justice and more reason, passionately embraced, might prevail.

The natural purpose of literature is indeed to portray things, not
as they are, but as they are seen by authors, who are, almost by
definition, persons more nervously sensitive than most of us, more
easily wounded by their fellow beings and their prosaic or gross
pursuits, alienated from society if not voluntary exiles, and often
anarchistic in their assertion of their jealous individualism. They
naturally are reluctant to conform and to bow to the ethical or social
mores prevailing around them. They voice their discontent with
more egotism but also with more forcefulness than the average
citizen. Wits have often remarked, only half-regretfully, that literature is almost inevitably made out of the misfortunes of others, at
times also out of the personal complexes, phobias, and sorrows of
the creator himself. He attempts to purge himself of the venom that
he has nurtured, of his abnormalities, even of his destructive and

criminal urges through instilling them into the makeup of those readers who identify themselves with his fictional characters. Émile Zola, once judged revoltingly sordid by English-speaking audiences, was compared by one of their critics to "a prosperous laundry, voraciously waiting for the dirty linen to be engulfed." He is now by far the novelist most widely read and enjoyed by the Russian masses and even by the once coy maidens and now liberated women of American colleges.

The revolutionary force of literature and of the arts stems from the presentation that they offer of life in the concrete, with life's tensions embodied in characters in conflict. "It dramatizes life," as the English critic F. C. Leavis put it, "so as to increase our awareness of its possibilities." It acts upon readers as a revenge upon and as escape from the repetitive mechanisms of nature and of the routine in our work. This has been especially true of literature since the French Revolution and the invasion by writers of almost all the fields of political and social speculation. The nineteenth-century novel in England, France, Russia, then subsequently in America was often the shrewdest and certainly the most effective form of social criticism.

In our own age, the concept of involved or committed literature, practiced in America during the era of the Great Depression and of the New Deal, has been codified by French theorists into a doctrine. It has not necessarily proved a boon to literature. But either as a doctrinaire creed espoused by writers trained in philosophy and dedicated to politics or as exemplified in imaginative creation, recent literature has greatly contributed to encouraging dissastisfaction with the present state of things in America and in Western Europe and in fostering receptivity to revolutionary moods.

To state such an obvious truth is in no way tantamount to endorsing the naive illusions and delusions of the potential revolutionaries of both continents, or of the even more revolutionary continents likely to explode tomorrow: Asia, Africa, and South America. Readers of Gramsci in Italy (1891–1937) or of Althusser in France, the two leading reinterpreters of Marxism in our time, admirers of Marcuse in America and of other heroes of the youth culture naturally suffer from the naiveté of all intellectuals: not having had much experience of an organizing or executive kind, they are not aware of the very narrow limits within which any states-man, revolutionary or counterrevolutionary, or merely a colorless middle-of-the-road leader can effect change. Only slowly and after a number of frustrating ordeals will it dawn upon them that the most thunderously acclaimed revolutions, the French, the Russian, the Fascist, or the Yugoslav one, have ultimately had to retain a great deal of the cadres that stood before them or to revert shame-lessly to what they had branded as outworn or as sheer evil. But at all times the young have had to commit their own errors, to fondle their own illusions, to assert their own discontent, without heeding the admonitions of their elders. That is their way, and a very healthy one in the long run, of proclaiming that all is not well in the world framed and controlled by their predecessors and that their coming into that world was not, after all, a vain and mechanical process.

There is hardly a problem in history more arduous than satis-factorily appraising the influence of ideas upon life. Where revolu-tions are concerned, we can state safely that most of them have been preceded by a marked disaffection from the prevailing regime acutely felt and bitterly proclaimed by intellectuals: Plato, Xeno-phon, Aristophanes, and many others among the Greeks; the "philo-sophes" and through them many aristocrats and middle-class people before the French Revolution of 1789; the liberals, reformers, and the critics of Czarist autocracy in Russia between 1905 and 1917. No reliable statistical means are available to tell us how many people had read Rousseau around 1770–89, or how widely read Marx, Nietzsche, Georges Sorel were in Europe in the early decades of the twentieth century. Such quantitative information is meaning-less in this realm of emotional intensity and of personal reaction to texts laden with explosive force. A few aphorisms culled at random, a striking formula or slogan taken from the *Social Contract* or the *Communist Manifesto* or from Nietzschean apocalyptic announce-ments of the death of God may suffice.

What some readers, inclined to violent protest and ready to distort the formula taken out of context, see in a doctrine, alone matters. If those readers happen to be journalists or professors invested with a vast potential influence upon their disciples, the impact of an appeal to drastic and violent change may become enormous. If the teaching of those thinkers or ideological writers moves to action men like Lenin, Ho Chi Minh, Mao Tse-tung, the fate of the world is suddenly at stake.

Historians of the French Revolution (which has not finished fascinating English and American scholars) have long pondered the enigmatic and crucial question: why did that revolution occur, of all countries, in France—the one up to then most attached to its kings, the most prosperous, the one in which the rate of economic progress had been (Britain perhaps excepted) the fastest—and not in the Low Countries, or the German principalities, or Austria, Italy, Spain? No simple answer can be offered. But it does seem probable that the chief explanation is that writers and thinkers in France alone had forcefully and with outstanding talent voiced their discontent with the inequalities, illogicalities, and privileges that they were denouncing. None of the defenders of religion and of the traditional monarchy happened to be endowed with a talent matching theirs for writing inflammatory prose, for dramatizing acts of injustice or absurdities of intolerance and fanaticism. What is more, those thinkers evolved, if not coherent systems such as the Socialist and Communist ones of the nineteenth century, at any rate a number of positive proposals for the reform of government, of justice, of the economy, of education.

Other factors played a part: the French nobility, unlike that of Britain, had become nonfunctional and had failed to ingratiate itself with the farmers and with the ascending middle class; the surge of population had produced a large number of young men better educated than ever before, nurtured in a literature of protest, but refused a chance to occupy positions commensurate with their merits.

Still, the one overarching factor that singled France out as the breeding land of the Revolution was that there alone had existed a critically constructive literature that, once the old regime crumbled, made it clear that new goals could be pursued and reached and new institutions framed. The organizing achievement of the first two French revolutionary assemblies, between 1789 and 1792, has never ceased to amaze the philosophically minded historian. Deeds had been prepared by thought. Ever since then, any French writer (and others in countries like Germany and Italy where the French upheaval was much admired) has looked upon himself as a forger of myths, that is, of novel ideas charged with explosive force and likely to be enacted in deeds. He believes he is pursuing the task once accomplished by the heralds and inspirers of the most portentous series of events in modern history.

If we focus our attention on the American scene, a first phenomenon is striking: in no other great country has the divorce between the literature produced by the most gifted writers and the main activity of the country (business, banking, industry, commerce, marketing, advertising) been more marked. One might probably count on the fingers of one hand the imaginative creators of eminence, read in the schools and the colleges as modern classics, who have been, not even supporters, but tolerant of the so-called establishment. Ever since 1930, college students have been exposed to the cynicism of "Sweeney Agonistes" and of Ezra Pound; to the more strident tunes of Ferlinghetti and Allen Ginsburg; to the satirical fiction of Sinclair Lewis; to *The Great Gatsby* and *The Catcher in the Rye* or Updike's and Cheever's pictures of suburbia, the gentler ironies of *Heaven's My Destination* or of John P. Marquand; to the drama of Tennessee Williams and of Edward Albee; to the pessimism of Steinbeck and of Dos Passos (they lost their talent when they ceased being pessimists); to that of the black writers, of Norman Mailer, and of almost all the American novels on World War II.

A parallel phenomenon has taken place in nontechnical sociological and economic writing, that is to say, in what has been addressed to nonspecialists and which has contributed much to mold the ideas of the college population since World War II. Not many of the textbooks and of the supplementary reading proposed to them seems to be favorable to conditions as they exist; the most influential of them, by John Kenneth Galbraith, by the most popular writers on the social sciences, who have placed their literary talent at the service of their disciplines (*The Organization Man, The Hidden Persuaders,* even *The Lonely Crowd*), criticizing the assumptions and the mores of American society, implicitly offer an alternative to what appears reprehensible; they have been understood by many young people as advocating a refusal to support an establishment that they judge to be based on injustice and on greed. A similar wave of self-indictment, after the Great Depression, had surged against many of the optimistic slogans of the America of Horatio Alger and of the Coolidge era. Many of the leading writers and intellectuals in the country, dismayed by the collapse of Wall Street and the frailty of the economy, turned against all the tenets of American culture and ethics. The New Deal took many of their strictures into account.

However, the great difference is that, between 1929 and 1938, it was still possible for those dissenters and malcontents to imagine that another country, with a different political system, might be a new promised land in which their imaginations could take refuge. Some pinned their hopes on Communist Russia and it took the ruthless Stalinist purges and the 1936–38 Moscow trials to disabuse them. Others invoked Gandhi and the legendary wisdom of the East or adopted Zen Buddhism. A few even believed for a time in the Nazi slogans of regeneracy and of "Force through Joy" and of a return to legendary Germanic myths. The more egoistic simply lived in Paris, Majorca, or Capri and washed their hands of an America that they derided as the land of Babbitt and as an air-conditioned nightmare.

Those illusions could no longer be entertained by the post-World War II generation. Russia, China, Nationalist India, and of course Americanized Western Europe cannot loom as a new Messiah even to the most starry-eyed Americans. They know that their fight has to be fought here and now, in their own country, and many cannot bring themselves to believe that the fight is worthwhile or can at present be won. They prefer to step aside and abdicate, take refuge in the oblivion provided by drugs, song, exclusive association with young people of their own age, and the cursing of all that their elders have accomplished.

Are we on the eve of a genuine revolution? Not certainly a political upheaval such as France, Russia, China have experienced, not unless unemployment reaches the levels attained in 1933–37 and the labor unions become altogether disaffected from the producers' and consumers' society as we know it. France in May 1968 seemed to fulfill all the conditions once predicted for a revolution; a strange conjunction between the rioting students, the industrial workers, and the employees of the tertiary sector of the economy brought the whole fabric of the country to a standstill. Over ten million people stopped working, many of them because the strike of all the means of transportation prevented them from repairing to their work. The conjuncture was most propitious for the Communists (who count fewer than half a million card-carrying members but receive the votes of almost a fourth of the electorate) to seize power. They refused to try. Their rank and file realized that their fate was bound up with that of capitalism and the consumer society and not at all with the utopian students whose slogans read: "Consume more, and you live less well" or "Merchandise is the opium of the people." The rift between the trade unions and the intellectuals has not been healed and will not be. Nor is it likely to be in the United States. A revolution that does not enjoy the support of organized labor is doomed to remain an impossibility.

Still another sort of revolution can and does take place that does not include the overthrow of institutions and the storming of the White House or of the Capitol. Like wars, revolutions begin in the minds and in the hearts of men. Only if and when the ruling classes have completely lost their confidence in themselves and are corroded by the teachings of their intellectual and spiritual leaders can a revolution occur and perhaps triumph. There are, however, other forms of revolution that are possible, even probable, at the present time: they could be more far-reaching than the New Deal was in 1933–36, or the Labor revolution in Britain in 1945, even more far-reaching than many so-called revolutions have been in lands of Western Europe and of South America. The role of literature and of the arts in bringing about dissatisfaction with America as she is cannot be underestimated, nor can the role of the universities, which Daniel Bell has declared are fast becoming more essential than business firms "as *the* significant social organization in society, . . . the major innovative institutions"[4] in our postindustrial society.

For a number of decades, until the impact of World War I and the disillusionment that followed it were felt, it may be fair to submit that traditionalism prevailed in the substance and in the methods of teaching in this country. The iconoclasts were few and far between. Nietzsche, Ibsen, G. B. Shaw, the Fabian socialists had been imported but had made only a shallow dent on the minds of the elite from private schools and Ivy League colleges. The fierce labor struggles and the repression by the strikebreakers employed by big firms did not profoundly move the humanists, the lawyers, and the Wall Street bankers trained in the centers of learning. The development of "Consciousness II," in Charles Reich's attractive but too simplistic categorizing—industrialization, commerce, and especially the corporate state, with business, government, and the military power welded into their diabolical alliance—occurred before and after World War II.

The first thirty years of the present century deserved being called "the age of confidence," and many a teacher or commencement orator upbraided it as an age of conformity. Only a few decades ago, in 1891, a writer who had given evidence of his boldness, William Dean Howells, refused to believe that there could ever exist an American Dostoevsky. Fascism and Hitlerism, then the upheaval of 1939–45 in Europe brought to American colleges and to American letters a number of intellectuals who had not been bred in the Anglo-Saxon reformist tradition, entertained no especial respect for empiricism, and found no rare virtue in "agreeing to disagree" and in eschewing the debates of ideas. To many of them, the word "revolution" was surrounded by a glamorous aura. They passed on some of their dogmatism and something of their revolutionary mystique to their American students.

The disaffection from religious conformity and religious faith reached a high watermark in the 1960's. Organized religion has had to concede this fact and to become permissive on matters of dogma and of sexual mores so as not to alienate the young altogether. The disappearance of Puritanism, however, has left a void in many a conscience and a sense of aimlessness, which afflict a number of them with lingering remorse. Their desperate effort to crush that lack of purpose often assumes the mask of exhibitionism and bravado. It is an affectation of innocence or a pathetic yearning for it rather than genuine freedom from all sense of sin.

With the weakening of traditional faith and even more with the prodigious advance in technology that incessantly runs the risk of overproduction, the once firmest basis of ethics and the most effective means of preserving morality, constituted by work, is crumbling down. Idleness was long condemned in many a saying of popular wisdom as the mother of all vices. *Robinson Crusoe* was required reading for young people because, instead of enjoying the untainted beauty of his remote island, the sturdy hero sets to work strenuously, to build and "to produce." He now appears to many as a ludicrous model, at best taken to heart by the Germanic race (with serious consequences for mankind) and by the new martyrs of the modern world, executives and big entrepreneurs. But the gospel of hard work, eventually to be rewarded by Divine Providence, and the superstition that there is a mysterious holiness attached to capitalism hold little sway with the young generations today. Growth has in itself no sacredness.

In a prophetic essay in 1930, "Economic Possibilities for Our Grandchildren,"[5] John Maynard Keynes was among the first to warn mankind that it was solving the economic problem that had caused it anguish for several thousand years. Technological unemployment was with us to stay and the relevant question would be: how to occupy our leisure in an age of abundance. We had been conditioned, particularly in Protestant countries, to strive rather than to enjoy. Henceforth, the trend would have to be reversed. In agriculture, in welfare, we have to reward those who do not choose to work or who are unable to do so. Laziness and following the Epicurean advice of *carpe diem* are perhaps the most beneficent attitudes. In literature, the love for money, which stood at the center of Balzac's fiction, greed, avarice, ruthless ambition have almost ceased to count among the motives of fictional and dramatic heroes. In our daily behavior, males on a vacation no longer proclaim, as ingrained conviction or soothing hypocrisy used to lead them to do, that they are merely "recharging their batteries" so as to return to their hard labor with renewed energy; they do not even take it for granted that they should take part in strenuous sports and rough it in order to soften their twinges of remorse at being away from their desks for a week or two.

The rules of economics and of business taught to the young strike many among our contemporaries as purely conventional and not at all in line with either the conditions prevailing today or the mood of the people in our postindustrial society. A high rate of growth is not necessarily a boon for an economy; it profits only a small group in a nation. Economic science envisages as the only goal of advanced countries an accumulation of material goods, and it extols a symbolic value, or more probably a mere shibboleth, the gross national product of a country. Politicians follow suit and boast of a 950 billion dollar G.N.P. in the United States. But a growing portion of that is devoted to remedying—very imperfectly at that— the evils caused by that gross national product, some of which, like deforestation, pollution of rivers and of the atmosphere, have at last become intolerable, thanks to literature. Meanwhile, parks, gardens, playgrounds are being neglected by the city, the state, the Federal authorities, and often by the mining companies, by General Electric, or Union Carbide, or the offshore oil companies. It is easy to rail at the young who own automobiles, musical and recording apparatus paid for by their hard-working parents or whose travel on charter planes is also financed by their progenitors. But such unconscious hypocrisy or illogic does not alter the fact that there no longer seems to be an imaginative and emotional glamor attached to the possession of goods. A profound change in our table of values, a Nietzschean *Umwertung aller Werte,* has taken place since 1950.

There have been precedents in other countries of a literature of protest and of gloom arising in the very midst of the country's prosperity in the economic sphere. Such was the England of Hardy and Gissing and Samuel Butler at the time of the late Victorian era and of Disraeli's political and imperial brilliance. Such was France during the Second Empire: while banks, railroads, commerce were thriving and capital was being exported and fructified, literally all the writers of talent (Baudelaire, Flaubert, Goncourt, Zola, Renan) portrayed the culture of their country as decadent, soulless, sold to speculators; the bourgeois became a perpetual butt for their sarcasms.

America is experiencing a similar phase of disaffection from its industry, commerce, and technology on the part of its men of letters, its educators, and, as a consequence, a large part of the youth. Any teacher who has lectured to college students on Kafka's characters enmeshed in the labyrinthine coils of bureaucracy and of an absurd society or on Arthur Miller's *Death of a Salesman* has shuddered at the eagerness with which the young identified themselves with those antiheroes reduced to hating their families, society, their monotonous antlike jobs, and themselves. It took little effort from their ideological and literary masters to convince them that anything connected with the Pentagon and the industrial-military complex is tainted with greed, or graft, and certainly with callousness toward individuals who refuse to be treated as objects, or as passive instruments of defoliation, of the bombing of children and of defenseless peasants, of pollution of the environment, perhaps of germ warfare. Passive as the modern public may have become, conditioned as it is by repetitious mass media and a glut of news, it is nevertheless morally revulsed when reading about the graft of politicians, the waste of the military machine, the hundred-dollar-a-plate dinners building up support for a Vice President ranting at the unruly and effete college youth. The disenchantment with technological societies, once predicted by Max Weber, is with us in the most advanced technological land. Success, measured in terms of money increments, concerns candidates for business positions much less than cultural and educational possibilities around their prospective residence and the quality of life that they and their families may enjoy.

The injustice inherent in all protests uttered by any young generation against its elders has unfortunately prevented the latter from conceding that much is valid in the strictures flung at them. It is regrettable for the people variously dubbed "establishment," "middle-class culture," "executives," or "conformists" that they have in this country no literature that portrays them as human beings, with their own anguish and torments and kind intentions, with their generosity and with their achievement; for it is they, who once believed with Carnegie that "wealth is a sacred trust," who saved Europe during and after World War II, who developed the research and the expensive technology that have made possible computer science, going to the moon, helping underprivileged nations. It is equally to be deplored that, engrossed in their pursuit of financial growth, of ever increased production and ever expanding demand artificially promoted, the former college graduates of twenty or thirty years ago have failed to keep up with the art and the literature now urging the disillusioned youth to revolt against the worship of quantity and of efficiency.

Capitalism as practiced in America is woefully misunderstood and maligned at home, with the disaffected youth, and abroad. It has never had a literature, not even an ideology expressed in philosophical and sociological terms, that did it justice. Worse, it has not even realized the potential power of ideas, of literature and the arts to endow a society with an adequate image of itself that it could project. A few of the business leaders have understood it: Clarence Randall, once the head of the Inland Steel Company in Chicago, who warned his own ilk that qualitative factors counted infinitely more in engineering, in commerce, in effecting technical innovations, than quantitative ones; or Walter Paepke, who died in 1960, the organizer of the Container Corporation of America, who commissioned art works, kept up with modern literature, developed the cultural center of Aspen, Colorado, and proclaimed that "Ideas are definitely more important to the preservation of our society and of our liberties than the pursuit of material gain." A third Chicagoan, Adlai Stevenson, warned his countrymen repeatedly against the neglect of humanistic and artistic values. "I pray," he told a Tufts College audience in 1962, "that the imagination we unlock for defense and arms and outer space may be unlocked as well for grace and beauty in our daily lives. As an economy, we need it. As a society, we shall perish without it."

The revolution that is now seething in the minds of the young and often the not-so-young may have little resemblance to the traditional political one with which the past has been familiar. Its consequences will be no less far-reaching for it; on the contrary, it will stand in less danger of being wrecked in a pitched battle with the powers that be and by a counterrevolution. It has established, for the first time in American history, antimilitarism in the psyche of our citizens, and the trend is irreversible. It has ingrained into many of us distrust of the politicians and apparently dug an unbridgeable credibility gap between Washington and the common man. It may well convince capitalism that it should advocate punishment (in the form of special taxes) for spoiling the environment and tax rebates and other rewards for companies, real estate, mining concerns that provide for cleanliness, beauty, art, silence in their communities. The country now counts nearly eleven million young persons in its colleges and probably some thirty or forty million college graduates. The yearning for beauty and for an enrichment of their inner lives burns in them, partly through the influence of literature and the arts. They are outraged to watch those humanistic ideals held up to them at school become irrelevant because they are disregarded in a society controlled by technocrats and bureaucrats. The ebullient prophet of *The Greening of America* expects that the world of "Consciousness II," with its political-military-industrial stifling alliance, will of itself collapse when the "greening," or resurrection, occurs and the young peacefully walk out of the trap. Professors of law are usually less optimistic, or naive.

But many signs point to the possibility of a renewal, even of a rebirth or palingenesis, once dreamt of in myth and religion. A *grande Peur,* a wave of irrational fear such as panicked the French provinces during the first year of the Revolution in 1789, now appears to have crept up on the Americans, who once had hoped to live without tragedy and to see the new Adam emerge in a new land. The collapse of "the American dream" is proclaimed with sarcasm, almost with bitter joy, by many. Yet the end to conventional optimism concerning the racial issues, the monstrous rearmament struggle among the super powers, the bungling by the government, the corrupt administration of the cities should give us encouragement. The conviction that, even in this age of technology and of prosperity, life can be tragic can become the source of a great good. "Dare ye be tragic and ye shall be redeemed," the prophet of Zarathustra exclaimed.

The pessimism of the young and of most of their intellectual leaders is fundamentally more constructive than the vapid optimism of yore. This country can no longer deem itself immune to the doubts and the anxieties and the problems of the old continents once left by those who sought liberty, security, and an end to theological and ideological feuds by crossing the Atlantic Ocean. It has achieved the miracle of building in America the greatest universities, the finest research institutes, the most highly developed science in the world. It now has to realize that such a splendid accomplishment inevitably means that both scientific and literary cultures imply obstinate questioning, dissent, unflinching universal criticism and stands therefore at variance with the traditional requirements of religious orthodoxy, of military discipline, of the promotion of business interests that disregard the need for idealism, for beauty, for a determined rejection of the inequalities and the inequities in our society.

One of the many intellectuals who have lately devoted much thought to endeavoring to predict and to prepare the future, Dennis Gabor, submitted that, if we usually fail ludicrously in predicting the future, we may at least invent it. Too many of us, persons over forty or fifty, "established" as the new term of insult goes and, some will say, "sclerosed," have not given up all hope of imagining a better future and of incorporating into an unsatisfactory and much maligned present what appears to our dreams most highly desirable in the future. We are not just on the verge but in the throes of a spiritual, intellectual, and scientific revolution. We owe an immense debt of gratitude to the young rebels around us for having awakened us to what is crumbling and grossly unjust in our lives and in our politics and economics. But the young, thus far, have mostly been negative in their criticism and have vented their indignation in rhetoric or in insults. They will only succeed in destroying what may be in need of destruction if they firmly know, through hard intellectual and imaginative thinking, what to replace it with. And they will not know it, and therefore they will not become truly constructive, unless their elders, from whom they secretly expect guidance, help them discover and perhaps install a new and revolutionary order.

The phrase "America's permanent revolution" was revived as a slogan by *Fortune Magazine* shortly after World War II. It must be revived again and not merely paid lip service to, but lived. In that sense, our thinking, in education, in science, in politics, in economics, and in business, must and will be revolutionary or it will not be. Success, and perhaps the salvation of this country and of the world, or irretrievable failure are equally possible and will probably be decided by the ideas and the courage of those who, between 1971 and 2000, will be called upon to face the revolutionary decisions to be made. May we, their elders, and especially the educators among us, help them make the constructive ones!

This essay (originally entitled "Arts, Letters and Ideas: Indicators of Change or Instruments of Revolution?") was first presented in an oral form at a symposium on "Change or Revolution" of the Institute of Life Insurance at Arden House in 1971. It subsequently appeared in the "Conference Report" of that Institute, 277 Park Avenue, New York. The editors are thanked for their kind permission to reprint.

## NOTES

1. Alexis De Tocqueville, *De Démocratie en Amerique,* Part 2, Chap. 21 (Paris, 1836).

2. G. E. Labrousse, *La Crise de l'Economie Francaise à la Fin de l'Ancien Régime et au Début de la Révolution,* Intro. (Paris: Presses Universitaries, 1944), p. 5.

3. Crane Brinton, *The Anatomy of Revolutions* (Englewood Cliffs: Prentice-Hall, 1952).

4. Daniel Bell, *Working Papers of the Commission on the Year 2000 of the American Academy of Arts and Sciences,* 2d meeting, Vol. 1 (1965-1966).

5. John Maynard Keynes, "Economic Possibilities for Our Grandchildren," *Essays in Persuasion* (New York: Norton, 1963).

# 4. Gide and Literary Influences

CRITICISM HAS BEEN RELATIVELY LENIENT to André Gide since his death, and even in his last twenty years, which produced few, if any, works of great stature. His successors may have wished to make amends for the long neglect in which Gide's early volumes had languished until he at last conquered the youth of several lands after World War I. They probably felt shy at taking advantage against him of the many weapons that he had, with masochistic humility, placed in the hands of his future detractors. The unevenness, even the wilful contradictoriness, of his many volumes and of his notes in his *Journals* provided almost every faction in the Parisian literary world with ammunition for its own fight. He could be claimed by the rebels but also by the classicists, by the Devil's advocates but also by the religious reformers, by the enthusiasts of Dostoevsky and by those of Racine. Few had distorted truth as subtly and had adorned themselves while maligning themselves as dexterously as the author of *La Porte étroite* and of *Et nunc manet in te,* and yet few had so steadily attempted to live by the motto of sincerity.

It is likely that the portion of his work falling into oblivion will be much larger for him than for Valéry and Claudel, certainly than for Proust. His plays will not stand the test of time; his lyrical confessions and litanies, in the *Nourritures terrestres* and even more so in the *Nouvelles Nourritures* and, obviously, in his notebooks signed André Walter, smack of artificiality. Three or four of his novels, at most, may continue to move posterity, and *Les Faux-Monnayeurs* may not be among those, except for technicians of the art of fiction

93

and readers curious of generous experiments. His traveler's evocation
of the North African scenery inspired him with his most sumptuous
yet unpretentious prose, unmatched by Chateaubriand, Gobineau,
Barrès, and other great names from the country of Europe that has
produced the most beautiful literature of travel. But Gide's eminence
as a critic has rarely been questioned. He reflected on literary problems, and not just those of form, at every period of his life. At the
core of many of his meditations lay the question of influences: those
which he had undergone and eagerly wanted to undergo, that which
he wished to wield over the young and over generations yet unborn.

Few questions are more vexing to the literary student.[1] Scholars
are by definition dedicated to reading extensively, often books that
nobody has read for a long time, in the hope of discovering the new
or the unacknowledged work. They have a retentive memory. They
have been trained to keep notes and to use them through complex
systems of cross references. It is hard for them to concede that those
authors whom we call imaginative have not spurred their imaginative creation through the perusal of everything that may have been
published around them. They declare it self-evident, if Baudelaire,
Mallarmé, or Gide happened to have had a few pages of theirs appear in a certain magazine, that they had read from A to Z all that
was published in that same magazine in the five or ten previous
years. They forget that few authors could afford to buy the reviews
that appeared, often unbeknownst to them, in the same city; that
libraries were in many cases poor or nonexistent; and that those
"creators" seldom led the secure lives of the academics. Their dreams
their loves, their sufferings, the artificial means with which they
sometimes stimulated a flagging inspiration, their links with artists,
often preferred by them to the *confrères* in the art of writing, mat-
tered more to them than information picked from books. As in the
sciences, there is such a thing in artistic and literary creation, in philosophy and in politics, as polygenesis, the almost simultaneous discovery of the same novelty or the parallel treatment of a new theme
or the use of a new technique. There is also such a thing as serendipi-
ty, as the scientists elegantly call it, from the fairy story of Ceylon in
which three princes of Serendip, looking for one thing, find another.

That unreadiness of omniscient scholars to accept that influences work mysteriously on the imagination of creators has caused a rift between them and the living writers whose works they scrutinize in order to establish *rapprochements.* Some writers, loved by the gods perhaps, die young; Camus was among them. Hemingway, Lermontov, Gide, Kafka, Jean Lorrain, and a score of others have variously been mentioned as sources for one detail or another of *L'Etranger* or *La Chute.* Others are too proud, or too uninterested, to grant any attention to source hunters: Hugo, whom some admirers or detractors viewed as having had, not only Virgil and the Bible, but the Kabbala and the Gnostics at his fingertips; or Malraux, who cares little if Worringer, Élie Faure, Focillon had already expressed views similar to his artistic inspiration. Others still can be bitter and sarcastic, and deride the sources ascribed to them, or attempt to mention impossible ones so as to throw the dissertation writers of the future on the wrong track.[2] The more modest ones, too gentle to contradict the scholars who scan every page of their writings, generously admit all the *rapprochements* sketched between themselves and their predecessors or contemporaries. Like Goethe, they know how mysteriously subterranean is the process of creation.[3] The Irish poet Yeats was one of these, and Richard Aldington blamed his "misplaced intellectual loyalty" overstressing what he might have drawn from a conversation, a passage, an allusion. So was Gide. Scholars of the future, who would collect the numerous allusions to a hundred authors of ten nations scattered in the *Journals* (Schopenhauer, Leibniz, Hebbel, Marlowe, Fielding, Meredith, Goncharov, et al.) and establish thereby a balance sheet of his debts to foreign writers, could produce a strange caricature of Gide's intellectual life. How often did he proclaim his rapture at beginning Keller's *Der Grüne Heinrich,* Meredith's *The Egoist,* a long poem by Browning, a novel by Arnold Bennett, or Conrad's *Under Western Eyes,* only to jot down, three weeks later, his irrepressible boredom with those books after the twentieth page. He owed them nothing, not even the impulse to create that the reading of a dull or poor book may instill in us. Gide was more candid than some in his avowal that some of Hardy's novels, those of George Gissing, which English friends had commended to him, those of Henry James, for which the French have seldom caught fire, the venerated but seldom perused *Elective Affinities* of

Goethe palled on him after a few hours. Apropos of Browning, whom he read assiduously between his fiftieth and his sixtieth year, he confessed (*Oeuvres complètes,* XIV, 70) his disappointment at reading some of Browning's poems while resting under his tent in the Congo: "There often is profit in not understanding perfectly. My imagination had lent generously to the mirage and painted my uncertainties with varied hues. Now that my sight is clearer, I am somewhat disappointed."

Gide's generosity in suggesting influences that his pliable nature might have undergone could be all the more misleading to future commentators since such a large portion of his writings is in the form of a diary. We are similarly tempted to exaggerate Montaigne's debt to Latin authors because his memory was filled with them and he quoted from them intemperately, and often pointlessly. The jotting down in a journal of the books one mechanically opened because they had been lent to us or purchased by chance while strolling along the *quais* is among the deceptive features of that genre of writing, which is much more often exterior than it is "intimate." The prestige of scholars, professors, and critics is such, even among the imaginative writers who have had the strongest reasons to distrust their judgment, that men of letters are naively proud to display the extent of their reading in order to rival professionals of criticism.

It is wise, in the case of Gide, deliberately to brush aside a great many names of foreign authors whom he read, sometimes even translated, but who cannot have counted for much in the molding of his thoughts and of his sensibility and even less in the evolution of his art. Among the ancients, Virgil alone appears to have appealed to him lastingly; but his Virgil is hardly ever that of the *Aeneid,* especially that of the last six books dearer to the *cognoscenti* than the tale of the fall of Troy or even than the descent to subterranean depths. Gide's Virgil, like Valéry's, reduces itself (if we omit apocryphal pieces from which he derived a convenient and enigmatic title) to that of the *Bucolics,* an expert but hardly original exercise in the pastoral manner of the Greeks. Hellenic myths haunted Gide more lastingly, and an excellent volume by Helen Watson-Williams has been devoted to Gide's treatment of them; but Gide hardly needed to

read Plato or the tragic poets or even Homer and Hesiod to dream
of Orpheus or Narcissus or Theseus.

His debt to medieval literature is likewise scant, even to Dante
and to Petrarch, occasionally quoted in Gide's youthful works or
read by one of his heroines. Beatrice is to chaste André Walter a
pre-Raphaelite apparition, a blessed damozel, "fior gittando di sopra
e dintorno," rather than the stern and harsh woman who upbraids
Dante for his failings in the thirtieth canto of *Purgatory*. As to many
moderns, the painters and sculptors of Italy altogether eclipsed her
men of letters, and none of the poets from Leopardi to D'Annunzio
enriched Gide's sensibility. Spanish writers are even more conspicuously absent from Gide's intellectual landscape. German thinkers
may have attracted him more powerfully at the time when, in his
middle twenties and still breathing the hothouse air of the symbolist
*cénacles,* he discovered philosophy: Schopenhauer most of all, probably, who had become well known in France after his death in 1860
and whom Wagner, then Nietzsche kept prominent in their writings
on philosophy and art; Fichte perhaps, although it is doubtful that
Gide seriously entered his more abstruse treaties. Lessing, easier to
read and more readily useful to a young man attempting to formulate his own aesthetics, through his *Laocoon* touched Gide's reflection more closely. Leibniz, I persist in believing despite an able attempt to link his *Nouveaux Essais sur l'entendement humain* with
Gidian aesthetic reflections,[4] impressed Gide's thought hardly at all;
he forced himself to read some pages of his as a penance or as a task,
to test his will. That may be deplored, since Leibniz is doubtless the
only original aesthetician in Europe in the two hundred years that
preceded Kant's *Critique of Judgment;* but systems of aesthetics and
the creation of beautiful works, literary or plastic, have very seldom
encountered a common meeting ground.

Young Gide, in the years 1889-92 (he left for North Africa in
1893), dissatisfied, like most young men of promise, with the fragmentary education he had received, was determined to supplement it
with systematic reading and to choose and control the influences to
which he would submit himself. In his touchingly adolescent plan-
ning of his life, his alter ego André Walter wrote: "Influences certainly mould us; one must therefore discriminate among them. Let

will power everywhere be in control. Make ourselves the one we
want to be. Let us select influences. Let everything be an education
to me." Later, granting freer play to his sense of humour, Gide offered to the young his counsel for bearing with much in life, and in
books, that palls on us: to repeat to ourselves that what bores us also
educates us. He plunged into Leibniz, into Kant, into Carlyle (out of
a sense of duty), into Spinoza, promised to himself to read the
Vedas, the Stoics, to wrestle with books of philosophy like Jacob
with the angel, and to emerge from the fight wounded and exhausted but victorious. Irony was soon to smile at those cerebral excesses
of André Walter; for less than two years after, in the *Voyage
d'Urien,* the narrator alludes to his female companion, Ellis, "seated
on a lawn under an apple tree, . . . eating a salad of scarole" and
reading the Kantian *Prolegomena to a future Metaphysics,* then,
lounging on the small boat, the *Theodicy* of Leibniz and some other
philosophical treatise, which he tears from her and throws into the
river.

In truth, however, the notion of influence, if distinct from the
passing impression left by some chance, or even disciplined, reading
of a variety of texts, should in the case of Gide only apply for five or
six writers (and among the French, to Stendhal, whose timidity and
self-defensive irony impressed the novelist of *Les Faux-Monnayeurs,*
perhaps regrettably): Goethe, Nietzsche, Dostoevsky, to a lesser extent Blake and Browning. Renée Lang has written a well-informed
and perceptive monograph on *Gide et la Pensée allemande* (Paris:
Egloff, 1949); we have since learned much more about the fortune
and the prestige of Nietzsche in France, although the comprehensive
book on that rich subject has not yet been attempted. The impregna-
tion of Gide by a certain Nietzscheism, seldom if ever obtained
through the reading of the original text and usually through ponder-
ing a few aphorisms and the more personal writings of the German
thinker, took place between 1892-94 and 1907: Gide postdated his
discovery of Nietzsche, perhaps through some vagueness in his recol-
lections, perhaps also because he wished to preserve the full originality of *L'Immoraliste.* The confusion, or the sin of omission, is a very
venial one. For, after the rebellion against conventional values that
his first North African trip had unleashed in him, the prolonged

Protestant adolescent was yearning for an iconoclastic message such as Nietzsche was to offer. He carried Nietzschean aspirations within himself. With revealing insight, he remarked in 1899 in one of the letters to Angèle that "those who understood Nietzsche best are the brains which had for a long time been prepared for him through some Protestantism or innate Jansenism." It was not, indeed, a lesson of "immoralism," or of exalting man above his mediocrity so that he might step in where the death of God had left a gap that Gide learned from Nietzsche; rather one of austere striving for difficulties in order to grow stronger through vanquishing them. Not *L'Immoraliste,* in which the ideological message is too obvious and the reasonings of Ménalque a caricature of Nietzscheism, but *Philoctète* and *La Porte étroite* bear the deepest imprint of the harsh teaching of the German philosopher. But such an impact cannot come under the term of literary influence. Nietzsche counted less for Gide, when all is said, than he did for Élie Faure, Saint-Exupéry, and above all Malraux. He encouraged the French Protestant, who had up to then curbed or repressed whole sides of his nature, to accept himself joyfully and to bring forth, with no qualms of remorse, the flowers whose seeds had been laid in him. Gide was still working on *L'Immoraliste* when, in 1900, two years before the novel appeared in print, he said in his thoughtful lecture on influences delivered in Brussels: "If great minds avidly seek influences, it is because certain of the riches which are theirs, filled with the intuitive and naive feeling of the immanent abundance of their being, they live in a joyful expectation of their new flowering."

The lifelong attraction that drew Gide to Goethe is a more complex affair. It did not rest, as far as texts reveal it, upon a very wide acquaintance with the very numerous volumes of Goethe. The novels, and even the theater of Goethe (although Gide was the prime mover of the publication of these dramatic works in French translation in the Pléiade collection), except for the two parts of *Faust,* counted but little. The conversations with Eckermann or with Müller, more easily accessible, must have been more often leafed through by Gide than the many literary, moral, aesthetic remarks scattered among Goethe's writings. The lyrical poems impressed Gide far more, particularly, as he told me once in a conversation, the *Roman*

*Elegies,* with their robust carnal paganism, and the *Divan,* in which the author of *Corydon* sniffed a certain emotion in the presence of male bodies. Psychoanalysts had not, when Gide became enraptured with the *Roman Elegies* (misquoting and misunderstanding their first line), probed into Goethe's long period of chastity (he was thirty-seven when he crossed the Alps on his Roman journey, after his assiduous but vain courting of Frau von Stein); Goethe's temperament was naturally less inhibited than that of young Gide, brought up among women. Still Gide sensed in Goethe's sexual liberation a move similar to his own, when he had broken free from a stern mother and a cramping Puritanical environment. Both had been born in a rather wealthy and dignified upper bourgeoisie; both revolted against that heritage, wishing, in Faust's words, to reconquer it in order to possess it all the better; both had gone through a period of burning romanticism, that of Goethe's early "Prometheus" and *Götz von Berlichingen,* that of *Les Nourritures terrestres.* But both also remained bourgeois to the core, even in their unconventionality, Goethe more reluctant to commit himself politically and more impatient of the disorderly youngsters (Hölderlin, Kleist, Beethoven himself) unable to transcend their romanticism and to rise to the serenity that prevails "über allen Gipfeln," Gide more prone to lavish praise on the young and to espouse a cause, then to forsake it as soon as his enthusiasm flagged. Their closest point of resemblance was probably in their untiring readiness to devour new works, to discover what the young were producing in Europe, and to give their admiration wholeheartedly. At eighty-two, on 8 May 1831 (he was to die ten months later), Goethe was still declaring, Soret reports: "I hate people who admire nothing, for I have spent my whole life admiring."

Dostoevsky entered into Gide's literary career when he had already composed his finest, if not his longest, novels (which he chooses to call "récits"). His whole conception of psychology, of man's relations to God and to the Devil, of the crushing of Western pride through self-humiliation, of the structure of the novel as polycentric and no longer unilinear like a tragedy was altered. It would be idle to discuss the results of Dostoevsky's tremendous impact on Gide. With all its faults, and the author's perverse attempt to impede credibility in his plot, in his characters, and in the paltry puppet in whom the novelist would like us to see Bernard's angel, with all that is un-Russian in a novel whose outlines are too sharply drawn, *Les Faux-Monnayeurs* is a pathetic but impressive failure, far preferable to the lean stories of Gide's old age from which all complexity and all density have disappeared: *L'Ecole des Femmes*, *Geneviève*, even *Thésée*.

Gide was too entirely different from Dostoevsky to borrow anything from him or to dream of creating characters similar to *The Idiot* or to *The Eternal Husband*, the two books for which, in a conversation with me in 1939, he expressed the most lasting admiraation. T. E. Lawrence (of Arabia), in an offhand remark quoted in the *Revue de littérature comparée* in January 1940 (p. 63), peremptorily declared Gide's volume on Dostoevsky to be no good. He added, not altogether unjustly, if sarcastically: "Gide tried to make Dostoevsky a Protestant and didn't get to grips with his real powers and depths. Few Frenchmen could. They are too dapper to feel as untidily and recklessly as the Russians." The Russian contemporaries of Dostoevsky, on the other hand, and for several years his political compatriots in Soviet Russia, had been horrified by the plunge into abysses of the former convict and suspected him of being a mad Frenchman or Belgian under Slavic disguise. Gide was shaken to his depths when he first read him, as he had been earlier, he told me, by *Anna Karenina* (in 1901) and by *The Kreuzer Sonata*. He had clearly been yearning for a type of novel in which man's relation to God (hence to the problem of evil, allowed by the Creator, and to that of freedom, granted by Him also, and a source of all misery and wickedness as well as the root of our dignity) would be paramount. English and French novelists had treated other relations, those of man and woman, of man and society, so often that the themes had become threadbare. Gide's desire was to abandon the cult of the will, which had been that of Corneille's characters and of Balzac's, of the revolutionary and Napoleonic heroes. Through bolder plunges into the contradictions of man and the abysses of sexuality and of self-abasement, a renovated French novel would attempt, like Dostoevsky's, to negate consistency of character, sense of honor ("a superfluous burden for the Russians," declares Karmazinov in *The De-*

*mons*), intellectual arrogance, and "pudeur." Unashamedly, the actors of those confused dramas would lay themselves spiritually bare before us. Many actions would have no causal explanation, not even an affective motive; they would be gratuitous promptings of the subconscious or of some malevolent force suddenly invading us. While Gide's whole view of life was altered by his admiration for those confessions in which the Russian characters humble themselves and while his resolve to complete and to publish *Si le grain ne meurt* and other later and smaller books of confession may have sprung from it, the imaginative works of Gide were hardly affected. Any imitation in the realm of psychology and of technique would have appeared like a caricature. His intelligence, even his sensibility were influenced, but hardly his imaginative power to create. That influence probably oppressed and crushed him.

Gide's willingness to undergo, even to seek, influences from writers of other nations may be traced to many causes, some of which only a psychologist or a psychoanalyst could delve into. He had more plasticity than his friend Valéry, almost as much desire to be affable and to please as Proust displayed, a broader curiosity for anything foreign than either of them, or than Péguy, Mauriac, Colette, Romains among those who were a few years younger than he. He also was impelled by a much more powerful urge to influence others than any other among the writers who, since Stendhal, have addressed themselves to posterity and asked to be judged "in appeal." The mysterious mechanism through which some artists survive and continue to puzzle and to disturb while the good that others do "is oft interred with their bones" puzzled Gide. A lasting annoyance with French nationalists, who only praised those authors whom they saw as belonging to a narrowly conceived "French tradition" and who distrusted anything foreign, lurked behind some of Gide's polemical pronouncements; hence a note of fervor and of missionary zeal in several of the Gidian utterances on the beneficence of broadening influences. All in all, the subject of literary influences is the one that inspired Gide in his most discriminating criticism. His main points may be made and dicussed here.

First of all, and parting company with many academic scholars who like to imagine all writers like Chateaubriand weaving lovely wreaths of sentences from earlier travel books or like Flaubert documenting his *Salammbô* or his *Tentation de Saint Antoine* exhaustively, Gide stressed bookish influences less than the lived and the living ones. His early intoxication with angelic or pre-Raphaelite poets and with quintessential builders of metaphysical castles in the clouds gave way, after his African trip and after his full acceptance of his own self as it was, to a relish for more concrete and carnal writers. He preferred the sensuous aspect of Keats to Shelley, the "raw meat" as he called it of Defoe and Fielding to Novalis' *Heinrich von Ofterdingen,* which he had once contemplated translating. Writers, like painters, frequently start from an earlier writer or artist whose work they wish to emulate, to redo, even to destroy; but in the process of creation, they add to that jumping board all that life has taught them. In 1927, Gide confided to his diary:

> I have long pondered that question of "influences" and I believe that very crude mistakes are committed on that subject. In literature that alone is really valid that life teaches us. All that is learned through books alone remains abstract and dead letter. Had I never met Dostoevsky, Nietzsche, Blake, Browning, I cannot believe that my work would have been any different. At best, they helped me unravel my thought. Perhaps not even that? I enjoyed hailing those in whom I recognized my thought. But that thought was mine, and I do not owe it to them.

Some random remarks made by Balzac or Tolstoy (the latter's attending, in a railway station, the post mortem medical examination of a woman who had thrown herself under a train after her lover had forsaken her, from which sprang the original idea of *Anna Karenina*) or in the *Journal* of Katherine Mansfield amply show what details may set the creative process moving in an artist. How much the observation of gestures, of clothes, of language idiosyncracies, gloated over by Proust in daily life, enriched his saga novel is clear from the many accounts given since his death by those who had met him in *salons,* at the Ritz, or in less glamorous establishments. A casual remark by a café waiter or by a charwoman, a thought expressed by a loved woman or by an indifferent friend, the sight of a picture in an exhibition often matter infinitely more to a crea-

tor than the reading of the masters. But since we are only able to
trace such sources in a few chance cases, the scholars prefer to over-
stress coincidences or encounters in earlier printed matter, which
their profession leads them to scan.

Gide's *Journals* are strewn with reflections on that process of influences which is central to literary originality. With only a little
systematization and without distorting the author's thought as it is
expressed through fragmentary *aperçus,* we may extract from these
Gidian pages a theory in defense of the true originality that influences, far from impairing, foster.

The most exterior type would be the poorly assimilated influence
that resorts to the plain imitation of a model. It was less frowned
upon in past ages when the concept of originality had not yet been
evolved. For the Roman poets who (except in satires and elegies)
imitated their Greek predecessors or for the Renaissance poets who
plundered the wealth of the ancients or that of the Italians, imitation
was a necessary, often a fecund, process. Maurice Scève, du Bellay,
Ronsard, Tristan L'Hermite practised it with no qualms of conscience.
The Spaniards, who were for several centuries the most vigorous
creators of forms and the most fertile inventors of plots in Europe,
and some Italians like Marino, who were subsequently maligned by
the very ones who had borrowed their clothes, were thus imitated
without scruple by the French. Since the imitators wrote in another
language and the "borrowers" stole themes and feelings, the harm
done was amply counterbalanced by the good.

The moderns, having made a fetish first of originality, then of
authenticity, do not lay themselves open quite so shamelessly as
their predecessors, from Scève to Chénier, to the charge of that imitation which is almost plagiarism. What was borrowed by Mallarmé
from Hugo (which is not inconsiderable), by Valéry from Mallarmé, by P. J. Jouve from Hölderlin, or by Maurois from English
biographers matters less than what they achieved with that material,
duly worked over and assimilated. Gide, the champion of sincerity,
quickly transcended the stage of imitation, and he was less adept
than Proust, probably less endowned with the gift of humorous mimi-
cry, to attempt pastiches. His many remarks on the elusive goal of
full sincerity, which he long wanted to pursue, had led him to fear

GIDE AND LITERARY INFLUENCES

literary imitation less than the more insidious imitation of ourselves
to which some laziness lures us in life. We fall into the same mold
of sentences, orally delivered or written. We write the same love letter ten times over to ten persons, utter the same complaints, end by
never experiencing what we express. On 11 June 1931, Gide noted
in his *Journals* that there lies the crucial difficulty: "There is a sincerity far more difficult to secure from ourselves and much more
rare, than that of expression. Certain beings go through life without
ever experiencing a truly sincere feeling; they do not even know what
it is. They only fancy that they love, hate, suffer. Even their death is
an imitation." It never occurs to these pallid creatures to strive after
the ideal that Gide set for himself and for his imaginary disciples,
after he had encountered it in Nietzsche (who had borrowed it himself from Pindar): "Werde wer du bist," "Become the one that thou
art."[5]

More mysterious and more effective is the influence through reaction and protest that we all undergo, but to which students of literature seldom grant its due. In the most closely tied circles (family,
class at school, literary group) we may have begun by modeling ourselves after some one dearly loved or deeply admired; more often
still we exacerbate our difference from our wives, our parents, our
teachers, our colleagues. A young man in particular, prone to ideali-
zation, soon perceives the flaws, the tricky calculations, the sordid
greed, the mental laziness of his father (Kafka is the most eloquent
example), of a party leader whom he comes to scorn, of a literary
master whose facile repetitiousness (Hugo, Renan late in their lives,
Anatole France) repels him. No religious influence was, in Mauriac's
case, as potent as the impact in reverse that moralizing, predicating
clerical novelists among his immediate predecessors (all members of
the French Academy), Bazin, Bordeaux, above all Bourget, exercised
on him. Never would he bring himself to distort life as they had
done and to laud Catholicism as bringing peace of mind. Gide himself, early, chose Barrès as his *bête noire,* ascribing far more impor-
tance than it deserved to the childish theses of the *déracinement,*
deriding him as the foe of any influence other than that of one's
native province and of the dead buried under its soil. Later, some of
his moves in life and perhaps even the tone of some of his writings

may have been prompted by his distaste for Cocteau ("le Comte de Passavant"), or by his fear of the scathing and destructive intellect of Valéry. Since the latter deflated at every opportunity the—to him —illusory balloon of sincerity in intimate confession, foreseeing perhaps the pitiless remarks on him that Valéry's notebooks would contain, Gide indulged his more indiscreet revelations and courted scandal, in the sense in which the word is used in St. Matthew.[6] Not without some humor and with that strange proneness to appear before a court as a martyr and be judged by his foes that made him attend the debate of *L'Union pour la Vérité* where he was incriminated, Gide even hinted once that in a sense his best disciple was his severests critic, Henri Massis. For, he added (*Oeuvres complètes,* XIII, 444), "the influence which I may have wished is an emancipating one: to encourage everyone toward his own direction and to help him differ as much as possible from me."

That influence which proceeds through an adverse reaction and not from sympathy is related to another manner of undergoing the impact of an embarrassing predecessor. We happen one day to hit in an author upon a development or an idea that we had thought by ourselves, but not yet expressed. What we deemed original, perhaps unique, then is not! With a little spitefulness, we silence that idea, which someone else had perhaps elaborated or expressed better, and we project in its place another aspect of our being. Thus it was that Gide (perhaps confusing dates or vague about the precise moment when the theme of *L'Immoraliste* tempted him) states somewhere that the novel was half composed when he became acquainted with Nietzsche's work. He seized the opportunity to lighten that part of the novel which would have discussed ideas too doctrinally and to put forward the pure narrative and the nature descriptions rather than the debate on transcending good and evil.

Critics in our time have wisely broadened our views about sources and influences; genetic criticism or, as it once was called, crenology has fewer devotees nowadays than among scholars who once concluded from any resemblance between two authors to an influence. The notion of families of minds, cutting across countries and centuries, is at least as valid, even if it offers wider scope to subjective conjectures and to arbitrary *rapprochements;* those may also be the most enlightening. Baudelaire and Browning probably never heard of each other and yet their pursuit of analysis in love, their blending of the past with the present and a note of tenderness make them, in spite of other differences, closer than were Baudelaire and the other English poet who celebrated him in "Ave atque vale." The same Baudelaire is closer to John Donne than to any French poet of the seventeenth century. Northrop Frye, in his book on Blake, *Fearful Symmetry,* hinted that "such a writer as Gérard de Nerval, who had presumably not read Blake, is much closer to him than Yeats, who edited him. In the study of Blake, it is the analogue that is important, not the source."

Gide did not fail to discover such affinities between himself and a certain foreign author of whom he was, at a certain time, in need, for spiritual even more than for literary reasons. In the years that followed his discovery of Dostoevsky and his obsession with the Devil in life and literature (1910-30), Blake helped Gide formulate some of his dilemmas about heaven and hell more strongly. It is doubtful that Gide read much by him outside the *Proverbs* and a few of the easier poems. Browning suited another mood in him, after 1930 and the Frenchman's ephemeral conversion to communism as the royal road to optimism and progress; he liked best several of Browning's last poems, which proclaimed that faith in life and in mankind: "La Saisiaz," "Prospice," "A Death in the Desert." From the last mentioned of those poems he extracted the line that he considered his motto as he was turning his back upon all churches and upon the pessimism that he viewed as inherent in Christianity: "I say that man was made to grow, not stop." In both those English poets, Gide was looking for a spiritual message more than for novel aesthetic emotions. All his life, he who coined an oft quoted quip on the peril of good feelings for literature, longed to read a message in the works that he admired and also to teach one—not necessarily a conventionally moral one—to others. He remarked, in his introduction to Goethe's theater in the Pléiade volume, how Goethe's genius was essentially didactic, bent on eliciting wisdom from life and even from life's follies and on transmitting that slowly acquired wisdom to others in his works.

More than a soothing similarity between them and himself, Gide was looking for an authorization in the books that he relished. With all the boldness that it took him to publish indiscreet books like his memoirs and the even more scandalous posthumous little volume on his wife, Gide long remained shy, vacillating, inclined to compromise. His intimate life was, for at least the first fifteen or twenty years of his married existence, one of concealment. He dared not, perhaps he could not, joyously proclaim "his own truth," even in France, any more than some of his English contemporaries could in the Great Britain of Oscar Wilde's trial. John Addington Symonds, A. E. Housman, Edmund Gosse, Lytton Strachey were just as reticent as Gide on their "peculiarity." Some of his literary enthusiasms, as he told me in a conversation in 1939 (for Marlowe's *Hero and Leander,* for Shakespeare's *Sonnets,* for Walt Whitman), had been prompted by the same curiosity about homosexuality and the same desire to justify it as had led him to write *Corydon,* the most significant of his books, he once hinted, but one of the most awkwardly didactic in the view of many readers. At other times, the similar interest that led him to pore over Winckelmann's volumes and over Platen's poetry was, he avowed to me, sadly disappointed. That influence through authorization may help, like the truth discovered and admitted on ourselves, make us free. It may also serve to cover up some sophistry or a display of our inability to come to terms with our inner difficulties and to purify ourselves of them in an artistic work. "How many secret Werthers," he wrote, "had remained unaware of themselves and waited only for the pistol shot of Werther to kill themselves!" The example of strong or great men may indeed wreck paltry weaklings, as that of Napoleon destroyed Raskolnikov and that of Goethe his pitiful followers lured to suicide. Once again, Gide retained the prudent wisdom of a moralist in the midst of his most disarming confessions. The *Proverbs* of Blake ravished him when he came across them: "If others had not been foolish, we should have been so." Fontenelle, in his curious *Disgression sur les anciens et les modernes,* had already submitted: "How many foolish things would we say, if they had not already been said!"

An influence, finally, can often prove also to be a stimulant and a confirmation. The question of the moral responsibility of literature, awkwardly posed and too dogmatically solved by Bourget and by

Brunetière in the years 1885–1900, could not fail to impress the Protestant youth. Gide remained strangely silent or uncommitted during the years of the Dreyfus trial, when Barrès was only one among many men of letters who lacked clear-sightedness and honesty, when Péguy and Blum discovered the duty of fighting with their pens for a new order that would not rest on injustice. Like Thomas Mann, Gide remained "unpolitical" very long, up to his fortieth year or later. Indeed, in the beginning of World War I, shaken by personal crises as much as by the plight of invaded France, Gide was for a time ready to join the Royalist group around Maurras, the least receptive to foreign influences and the least "Gidian" of Frenchmen. He soon withdrew, as he withdrew also at that time from the temptation of a conversion to Catholicism, which had just proved a refuge for several of his friends. The lucid sight of his converted friends, notably Francis Jammes, and the imperiousness of a great converter, Claudel, kept him from imitating Ghéon or Copeau. Dostoevsky, Blake, other authors from England, Russia, and France then enlightened him on his inner turmoil and confirmed him in the way that, with La Symphonie pastorale (1919) and after, was to remain his: unbelief, despiritualization perhaps, interpretation of Christ's message separated from that of Saint Paul and of the established Church. Literary influences confirmed him in what he wished to be. Works of literature, of art, of music may thus have the power to reveal us anew to our own selves. At thirty-one, in his Brussels lecture on influence in literature, Gide already had poetically declared of influences:

> They have been compared to all kinds of mirrors which would show to us, not what we are already in fact, but what we are latently.
> "Ce frère intérieur que tu n'es pas encore," said Henri de Régnier. I would compare them more precisely to that prince, in one of Maeterlinck's plays, who comes to wake up princesses. How many slumbering princesses we carry in ourselves, unknown to us, waiting for a contact, a harmonious chord, a word to awaken them.

The whole critical work of Gide, and in a sense the whole of his work viewed in depth, constitutes an apology for influences, eagerly

sought, intelligently assimilated, and enabling him who has been enriched by them to influence others in his turn.

From the early *Nourritures terrestres* to *Les Faux-Monnayeurs,*
even to the allusions implicit in his later treatment of Hellenic
themes,[7] Gide never regretted or renounced his iconoclastic exclamation: "I hate you, families!" The families thus indicted stood for all
that is too close to us, all the possessions that in the end possess him
who thinks he is their possessor. The only tireless traveler in the
group of authors that counted many stay-at-home Frenchmen
(Proust, Valéry, Péguy, Colette, Mauriac), except for the diplomat
Claudel, Gide needed to see his own country and its traditions with
foreign eyes to confirm himself in his preference for Montaigne,
Racine, Baudelaire, Poussin, even for the Frenchified Pole Chopin,
only after having explored the writers and the artists of other
lands. The vociferous group of nationalists who, between 1908
and 1914 and even later, gathered around rightist literary magazines jealous of *La Nouvelle Revue française* annoyed Gide all
the more because some of his former friends, then turned into
harsh critics, were among them. They were so fearful of losing their
personalities, if not their souls, through opening themselves to currents from abroad and through admiring foreign authors that Gide
suspected them of having very puny personalities indeed and very
pallid souls. Such timorous prudence is a confession of weakness,
as, later, the expulsion or the subsequent destruction of Jews by Hit-
lerian Germany was tantamount to an avowal of fear and of inferior-
ity. "Our only real triumphs are over what we have assimilated,"
noted Gide in his *Journals* in May 1922. Minorities, ethnic, intellectual, like dissensions, can result in a substantial gain for the culture
that has youth and vigor enough to be enriched by variety. Gide
yielded to some restlessness when he set out for travels to lands most
different from the narrow and complacently self-centered Parisian
circles, but also to his irrepressible hunger for all that was strange.
In his volume of memoirs, he noted with some charm:

> I can do no better than compare exoticism to the queen of Sheba
> who came to see Solomon "to prove him with hard questions." It
> cannot be helped. There are beings which become enamoured with

what resembles them, others with what is different. I am among
the latter. Strangeness beckons to me, just as anything familiar
displeases me.

Foreign influences are beneficent because they are novel, strange,
enigmatic, but also because they are the slope up which we must
climb, a source of difficulty, and an antidote against mental apathy
or the slumber of the soul. Their value is extolled by Gide because
it is, at one and the same time, aesthetic and ethical. In the most
severe and the most beautiful of his undramatic dramas, *Philoctète,*
he pronounced: "What we undertake above our strength, that is
what I call virtue," French education steeps a French child so completely in the classics in his own language that Descartes, La Fon-
taine, Hugo, and Verlaine have penetrated into the marrow of his
bones. There is scant merit for him in feeling their charm spontaneously, and he even becomes convinced that their secret cannot
be deciphered by foreigners. In contrast with those neatly drawn,
elegantly kept, orderly French gardens, Shakespeare, Dostoevsky,
Whitman appear at first like uncouth monsters. Foreign readings
offer to a Frenchman the benefit of the Baudelairian "charms of
horror" and not conventional and comforting orderliness. "All that
to me is charming is also hostile," Gide said in his introduction to
another disconcerting drama, *Saül.*

Periodically, after the impulse provided by a new creative movement (be it romanticism, naturalism, symbolism, surrealism) has
died down, French literature undergoes a crisis of self-doubt. It is
tired of boldness and experimentation; it wishes to stress technique
and form, to polish the stones already quarried by enterprising predecessors, and chisel the trees uprooted by others in some dark for-
est. Without the recourse to foreign influences and the borrowing
of new sap, French literature would be in danger of being sclerosed.
In his lecture on Verhaeren, in 1920, Gide denounced that peril in
forceful terms:

> In France, form triumphs always and over everything, because
> the French people are the most artistic in Europe; and the peril . . .
> is that form comes to be frozen and to turn into a formula. A
> sclerosis would ensue, if, periodically, what nationalists look upon

as a foreign virus did not intrude and provoke a violent palpitation, through which our poetry becomes all revivified.

The most thoroughly and widely influenced writer often happens to be also the most original; such is the first conclusion, so often verified in the past with Chaucer and Molière, proposed by Gide's critical reflection. That nation has intellectually retained its youth whose appetite can devour everything and whose stomach can assimilate it just as easily. In a curious passage left out from the final version of *Si le grain ne meurt,* but quoted in Charles du Bos's *Dialogue avec André Gide* (1929, p. 69), Gide asserted, in regard to foreign influences, that "a truly French brain is capable of tolerating all of them. . . . All naturally stems from the digestive power of the brain. Mine could have digested stones."

And a second conclusion might doubtless be formulated thus: the most cosmopolitan of writers is also the most national one, and all the more universal since he is more national. Stendhal, Baudelaire, Proust (Claudel himself, whom a number of French nationalists had deemed unworthy of being French), Rilke, who was so powerfully impressed by Rodin, Cézanne, Valéry, the Dane Jacobsen, by Russian culture, Pushkin fascinated by Chénier, Byron and others were all and have remained deeply national in spite of having been (probably *because* they had been) most thoroughly permeated by outside influences. The nationalist author is anxious to stress what in him differs from others and to express what he imagines other literatures to conceal or to be incapable of expressing; the truly national author is he who, behind exterior differences, expresses what is broadly human. Klaus Mann, who admired Gide even more than he did his own father, declared in November 1938 in an article in *Les Cahiers du Sud:* "Of all the French writers, Gide is the one who offers the largest number of English and German traits." The assertion goes too far and can hardly be sustained. I would prefer to submit that, having rubbed himself against three or four literatures, penetrated deeply into half a dozen foreign authors, Gide merely became more French in the broad and traditional sense, that is, more tolerant, more generous, more human than he might otherwise have been if he had allowed himself to be terrified by influences.

"Gide and Literary Influences" appeared in 1970 in *The Australian Journal of French Studies,* Vol. 7, Nos. 1–2, published by the Hawthorn Press for Monash University. The editor is gratefully thanked here for permission to reprint.

## NOTES

1. I treated this question (Gide's attitude to literary influences) earlier, in an essay in French published during World War II in *Modern Language Notes* (Baltimore), 57, No. 2 (Nov. 1942). Some of the same views are presented here.

2. Jules Romains, prefacing in 1925 a new edition of his verse, *La Vie Unanime,* denied having undergone the influence of Walt Whitman and of the sociologist Durkheim and acknowledged the nobler one of Hugo, Goethe, and . . . Homer. Such a *rapprochement* is naturally flattering. Pierre Reverdy, in *Le Gant de Crin,* Jules Supervielle in humorous statements to questioners have, more generously, acknowledged influences on their work, but insisted rightly that their role in the creative process is extremely subtle and that influence has nothing in common with plagiarism. The poet Francis Thompson, with fewer circumlocutions, declared poetry to be a rootedly immoral art, in which success excuses everything. "A great poet may plagiarize to his heart's content, because he plagiarizes well."

3. On 12 May 1825, Eckermann reports Goethe's sensible avowal: "If I could give an account of all that I owe to great predecessors and contemporaries, there would remain only a small balance in my favour." On 16 December 1828, Goethe returned to the same annoyance caused in him by source hunters who question a poet's originality: "we might as well question a strong man about the oxen, sheep and swine which he has eaten and which had made him strong. . . . To enumerate the sources of my culture would be an endless as well as a useless task."

4. By Vinio Rossi, *Gide, The Evolution of an Aesthetic,* Rutgers University Press, 1967, pp. 104–08.

5. I have discussed the formula, and the theme, further in the chapter on "Gide Martyr and Hero of Sincerity" in my volume *Literature and Sincerity,* Yale University Press, 1963.

6. The English Bible translates it as "offence." "Woe to that man by whom the offence cometh!" which follows: "For it must needs be that

offences come." Nietzsche has remarked, and Gide probably remembered it, for he confided to me that *The Will to Power,* in which the sentence occurs, was his favourite among Nietzschean works: "Socrates, I have to confess, is so close to me that I am incessantly struggling against him."
7. Theseus is certainly not a model of a good "paterfamilias" and Orpheus, in the pseudo-Virgilian poem from which Gide borrowed the title of his cruel little book on his deceased wife, turned back deliberately to look at Eurydice and send her back to hell thereby.

# 5. Claudel and the French Literary Tradition

"How very French!" Every Frenchman living abroad has, at some time or other, been peeved by that exclamation, on the occasion of some witty or risqué remark, of a logical argument, of a certain taste in food or dress in which he fancied he was being cleverly original. The writers born around 1870 whose output and prestige dominated the literature of 1920–30 in France were all but one, and in praise or blame, called "very French": Valéry for the sharpness of his intellect and his eulogies of Descartes, Gide for the subtle restraint of his style and for his unwearied probing into his own ego, Proust for his concentration on the Parisian scene and his unmasking of social hypocrisy, Péguy for his patriotism and his distrust of all that was foreign to the land of Joan of Arc, Colette for her passion for the soil of France and for her stylistic virtuosity. Claudel alone set the scene of his dramas in strange and remote countries, drew some of his inspiration from the Old Testament, often unfamiliar to Catholic and humanistic France, spurned the traditional constraints of French verse and even of French prose, spent many years on continents, Asiatic and American, where none of the others ventured. He puzzled foreign observers and readers, who found that he failed to correspond to their notion of a rational, sensuous, subtle, Voltairian Frenchman. He puzzled many of his countrymen even more: for years, the charge that irked Claudel most, among the numerous gibes flung at him by hostile critics, was the one that declared him "un-French" and suspected him of being afflicted with a Germanic imagination and with a barbaric urge to wreck the traditions of the clear French language.

It is of course a childish enterprise to weigh the greater or lesser degree of "Frenchiness" (or of "Britishness" or of "Hispanidad") of any artist, just as it is to pin down as characteristically "Jewish" some features of Soutine or of Chagall and as Spanish or Catalan other traits of Picasso, Gris, or Miró. The most national of writers are often those who have been most widely influenced by foreign models, from Chaucer and Molière down to Goethe, Yeats, Gide, or Wallace Stevens. Claudel grew up at a time when Comparative Literature as a discipline had not yet penetrated education at the secondary or even at the more advanced stages; foreign languages had won a modest place in the syllabi of lycé, but their status was deemed much inferior to that of Latin and Greek. Even the nineteenth-century French authors, Victor Hugo excepted (and limited to his least original poems), were, if at all, grudgingly accepted by the teachers and by most academic critics. The zest with which Flaubert, Baudelaire, Verlaine were, in the 1880's, suddenly discovered by the youth, liberated from the conventional admiration for the French classics when they left the lycée, was all the keener. A touch of romance similarly made reading Shakespeare and Poe, and listening to Wagner, an exciting as well as an exotic experience for the teenagers. Gide, one year younger than Claudel, was drawn first to Dante, to Goethe, and to Nietzsche between his seventeenth and his thirtieth years, then to Blake and Dostoevsky. Valéry, four years younger and the one who then knew the English language best of all of them, always remained cool to Shakespeare, whose metaphorical luxuriance and verbal lavishness almost oppressed him; he never seems to have been drawn to any of the English poets and reserved his unbounded admiration for Poe, "my great and favorite genius. . . . the supernatural and magical poet, the most artistic one of the century," as he declared to Mallarmé in 1890 and later to Dr. Mondor. Poe's *Eureka* never ceased to fascinate fastidious and skeptical Valéry as a profound cosmological epic. Claudel, the only one of the renowned French admirers of Poe to set foot on the American continent, indeed to live in Poe's native city, Boston, remained throughout the years as warm in his admiration for him—one of the supreme poets in the English language, in his eyes—as it had been customary to be around 1890 in Mallarmé's circle. On 18 April 1909, in a letter to André Suarès, he defended the American storyteller, the poet, and even the thinker in Poe, which may seem all the more surprising since Claudel was composing some of those long poems, and in a sense, didactic ones, which had been vigorously condemned by the theoretician of "the poetic principle." His stories, wrote Claudel,

> convey most fully the sensation of America, either superficial with her taste for the sensational or profound, of the land accustomed to the darkness which so long enshrouded it and which man has not yet fully succeeded in exorcising. Poe is a white man who has undergone the spell of the demons of solitude. His case is that of Hawthorne, with talent thrown in in addition. He is also the author of "Ulalume" and of a few other poems, the most beautiful in English along with those of Keats; and he is the builder of that admirable poem, *Eureka*. He was a deep heart and a great intellect.

As he left his Parisian lycée in 1885 and started his studies in law and political science, and being ready for the overwhelming impact that the reading of Rimbaud's *Illuminations* was to have upon him the following year, the teenager Claudel impatiently shrugged off all the literary luggage that had been piled up upon his shoulders and threw himself, as he phrases it in his "improvised memoirs" of 1951, on Shakespeare. For a year or two, he learned English from his plays, with the help of French translations and of an English-French dictionary. Shakespeare's influence, he proclaimed sixty years later, is felt throughout his first complete drama, *Tête d'or* (1889), in the strangeness of the composition, the movement, the range of the imagery. Claudel, in truth, magnifies that Shakespearean influence overmuch, with the same overgenerous or misplaced loyalty that Yeats often evinced when the Irish poet likewise pointed to the extent of his debt to those ancient and French writers whom he called "the builders of his soul." The very few early admirers of Claudel's drama, Maeterlinck and, later, a young student of English, Alain-Fournier, writing to his friend Rivière, also exaggerated the similarities between Claudel and Shakespeare. What French writer would not be immensely proud to see his name thus linked with that of the most towering genius in literature? Claudel's originality, when he entered the world of letters, lay in his appreciation of Shakespeare's poetical comedies even more than of his tragedies; for Shakespeare's comedies, except perhaps for *Twelfth Night,* have never proved unquestioningly successful across the Channel. *Midsummer Night's Dream* was performed, in a French version, at the Odéon theater, near which Claudel lived, in 1886 and seems to have left its imprint upon *L'Endormie,* his fanciful, fairylike, and at the same time grotesque early play, which Pierre Brunel, the best scholar on the whole question of Claudel's relationship to Shakespeare, assigns to the year 1887. Much later, Claudel bestowed very high praise upon Shakespeare's last comedies, seldom unreservedly admired abroad: *Cymbeline, A Winter's Tale,* and even *Pericles.* He clearly had them in mind when he composed some of the strangest scenes in *Le Soulier de Satin.* Assured, as he drew close to fifty or sixty, of his place in literature, even if adverse critics and members of the Academy were still ostracizing him, the ambassador-poet knew that he could enjoy the privilege of old age and throw to the winds all the conventional rules of prosaic order and common sense. Shakespeare had perhaps felt likewise in his last years. Claudel, moreover, who professed not to understand what a "cosmic poet" was or meant and disliked being thus characterized, repeatedly maintained that he would rather be called a "comic" poet. The blending of comedy with tragedy had, naturally, been advocated and practised in France long before Claudel, most conspicuously by Hugo, whom Claudel resembled far more than he would ever admit. In Hugo, as in Claudel, that violation of the once sacrosanct rule of the neat separation of the two genres owed not a little to the great Shakespearean models.

In those same years of intoxication with Shakespeare, probably in 1886, it seems that young Claudel witnessed a performance of *Hamlet,* in Claretie's translation. He profoundly disliked the impersonation of the Danish prince by the then famous Mounet-Sully and, unlike Mallarmé and Laforgue, who sympathized with Hamlet's vacillations and with his cultivation of dream, Claudel refused to identify with the tormented and hesitant hero. "One is not in the created world to be understood, but to vanquish it; it is possible, and natural, to triumph in that struggle." Such were the aging poet's imperious words to his questioner Jean Amrouche. One of the most percipient commentators on Claudel, Maurice Blanchot, did not hesitate to see in him a Nietzschean, a man impelled by an indomitable will to power. Tête d'or, Rodrigue, and Turelure himself, with whom Claudel, half-humorously, marked his affinity, are indeed conquering temperaments, unimpeded by Hamletism.

A few years later, in 1900, a translation of *Hamlet* appeared in Paris. It was the work of two men, one of whom, Marcel Schwob, had been at school with Claudel in Paris and had remained his close friend. Schwob, a voracious reader, an enthusiast of Stevenson, probably did much to incite Claudel to read Marlowe, Webster, and other contemporaries of Shakespeare, whom two well-informed and judicious volumes by Alfred Mézières had already presented to the French public. Claudel sent Schwob a very penetrating letter, thanking him for the gift of his translation, offering keen remarks on the art of translation, and commenting on the central problem of *Hamlet* with much incisiveness. His letter, published in the appendix of *Marcel Schwob et son temps* (1927) by Pierre Champion, is, in its own way, as significant a text for the elucidation of *Hamlet* as Goethe's well-known pages in *Wilhelm Meister*. Claudel, at his best, is among the most perceptive creator-critics in the whole range of French literature:

> From the very first, Hamlet dimly realizes that his own death is the condition of the murderer's death, that his fate is bound up with that of the king, not out of necessity, but through a kind of dark bond: hence the source of his terrors and of his hesitation. A minister of death, only through his own death can he perform his self-assigned task. Hence also his madness, which is but the irony of someone already freed from his fate, the sarcasm of the protagonist who, with a shrewd eye, watches the other characters conscientiously involved in a plot whose catastrophe, envisaged by him alone, concerns them all. . . . Shakespeare composed the drama of death, depicted the anguish of souls who cannot just achieve death by themselves, but must forge their mutual bonds more firmly and make, out of their diverse fates, one single knot which one single blow will cut off.

It seems likely that, led by the enthusiasm of Marcel Schwob, young Claudel read other Elizabethan dramatists in those years of romantic rebelliousness against his classical French education. Parallels have been sketched between *Tête d'or,* conquering Europe and rushing toward Asia, and *Tamburlaine,* Marlowe's drama of strange and fierce violence. An English diplomat, Robert Nichols, who knew Claudel in Japan, is said to have been much impressed by the French ambassador's familiarity with Elizabethan dramatists usually known, in France, only to specialists: Beaumont and Fletcher, Webster, Massinger. That testimony, however, later reported by a commentator and admirer of Claudel, Georges Cattaui, is hardly decisive. Claudel may have read some of those dramas, or read about them, around his twenty-fifth year; but their utter lack of Christian awareness, their gruesome excesses held little sway over him, and they exercised no perceptible influence over his works, not any more than the Spanish dramatists of the Golden Age, whose fertility of invention elicited from him some lukewarm praise but who failed to impress even the author of *Le Soulier de Satin.* In truth, the evolution of Claudel's taste and his growing insistence on a Catholic, even more than on a Christian, attitude in the works to which he granted his admiration ungrudgingly, were, after 1900 or so, to lead him farther and farther away from English literature. His travels seldom took him to Britain. Even as a diplomat, active or retired, he left out England from his dreams of a European union that punctiliously included Franco's Spain. Britain was to him the land of the Protestants, whom he delighted in mocking, and of the Puritans. Milton, even in his biblical and lyrical drama on Samson, never seems to have touched him in the least. The English novel of the nineteenth century likewise left him cold, even that of the Brontë sisters and of Thomas Hardy, in which he might have detected the tragic evidence of God's absence. In 1942, he wrote to his friend Louis Gillet, who was one of Joyce's early admirers, a violent letter of horror and dislike for the Irish author whom, he avowed in his *Journal,* he had refused to read. That was not the sole occasion on which he wilfully cultivated injustice in his literary judgments and threw charity to the winds. In a brief article on Péguy, in February 1939, he quoted a critic's remark to the effect that French Catholic writers of the last century, from de Maistre to Bloy, had been conspiculously devoid of charity and of humility. Pascal, and even the Fathers of the Church, had provided them with models of unforgiveness, he added; and since the Catholic Church stands like a besieged citadel in our time, the besieged ones must resort to vituperation and shout their indignation. Claudel, however, could also be diplomatic and conciliatory, and he never felt any qualms of conscience about contradicting himself. When in June 1939 he addressed an audience at Cambridge University, which was bestowing an honorary degree upon him, he praised the wealth and the greatness of English literature, compared English lyrical poets to the finest in classical antiquity, and even confessed to a taste for Thomas Hardy, "whose bitter sweetness held a fortifying virtue for him" (*Oeuvres en Prose,* Pléiade, 1965, pp. 1324–25).

Nor did Claudel feel drawn to the English lyricists of the nineteenth century or to those of his own age. A romantic in spite of himself, preferring inspiration to patient and intellectual poetical alchemy, verbal abundance and rich imagery to conciseness and restraint, he might have discovered some affinities between his own lyricism and that of Blake, Wordsworth, Byron, Shelley. But, questioned by myself when I was writing a book on *Shelley et la France,* subsequently published in 1935, Claudel strongly voiced his distaste for what in Shelley's poetry is dreamy, soft, vague, effeminate. He much preferred the sensuousness of Keats. In other pronouncements of his, especially apropos of Richard Wagner in 1926, he branded all that English poetry of the early nineteenth century as "invaded by a Satanic emanation." How could Shelley, that "milky character, voluntarily imprison himself for months in the atmosphere of the Cenci?" Curiously enough, he excepted two English Catholic poets from that sweeping condemnation: Francis Thompson, an admirer of Shelley and a mystic hunted by "the hound of heaven" as well as by his own frailty, an accursed poet at times reminiscent of Verlaine, and Coventry Patmore, a convert to Catholicism who courageously and steadfastly sang the bliss of married life. Claudel, not always sensitive to the prosaic conventionality that often mars Patmore's poetry or to the stilted exaltation of some of Thompson's odes, translated into French some of their poems. Patmore, who died in 1896 without having an eminent place among the English poets acclaimed in their own country, had been revealed to Claudel, then at the Benedictine abbey of Solesmes and struggling with himself (and with God, as he testified) in his desire to become a monk, by an English convert to the Catholic faith, Algar Thorold. A whole volume by one of the fervent Claudelians of our time, Alexandre Maurocordato, was written in 1964 on Patmore's influence on Claudel and on the merits of the French poet as a translator. Even more bewildering, however, is the interest that Claudel bore for violently romantic, satanic, and self-tortured Thomas Lovell Beddoes, a homosexual who led a wretched existence away from his native England and, at forty-six, ended his life through poison. His best achievement, *Death's Jest-Book,* is the most macabre and the bitterest pessimistic drama produced in England since Ford and Webster or since Otway's *Venice Preserved* (1682), a drama that had haunted Balzac's imagination.

American letters, Poe excepted and, for a brief while, Hawthorne, apparently left Claudel indifferent. Some of his contemporaries among the young *epigoni* of the symbolists, around 1890–95, and later Gide, had acclaimed Walt Whitman and perhaps found models of liberated, or polymorphous, verse in his long, uneven lines. Claudel, wisely, knew better and held to his own theories about the iambic meter as essential to dramatic verse and to the physiological basis of his own "verset." Later still, when living in Washington and forced by his ambassadorial functions to travel across the country, he seems to have evidenced no interest in the literary renaissance that gave America O'Neill, Dreiser, Faulkner, and none in the fiction of Henry James. He doubtless could have felt horrified by their (genuine or inverted) Puritanism and by their obsession with sex and with Freudianism. The renaissance of American poetry, attributed in part by some critics to the impact of the French symbolists whom Yeats, Pound, Eliot praised generously, passed by the ambassador-poet, who had discovered his own vocation through Rimbaud and Mallarmé and remained a lifelong admirer of Verlaine.

His diplomatic career took Claudel to Prague (with frequent trips to Vienna) in 1910, then to Frankfurt and to Hamburg until August 1914. He had studied some German at school, although he never became fluent in the language. German translators were the first to present some of his plays to audiences across the Rhine, when French theaters were still keeping shy of Claudel's lyrical or supposedly unclassical dramas; directors of great fame, Max Reinhardt or Piscator, were inclined to stage his plays while the French theatrical producers feared him or sneered at him. The thinkers and the philosophy teachers in France, in the years 1900–14, hailed Kant, Schopenhauer, Nietzsche as their inspirers. One of them, Boutroux, was fond of quoting Goethe in every one of his books. Scandinavian plays appeared to the audiences of the "Théâtre de l'Oeuvre" as the symbolist plays par excellence and the fervor of the French elites was reserved for Ibsen, Strindberg, or for Tolstoy's *Power of Darkness*.

Claudel remained unmoved, or stubbornly hostile. Few charges irked him more than those of the ponderous critic of *Le Temps*, Paul Souday, who had found his writing as monstrously un-French, as if it were translated from German or, worse still, "some Ongro-Finnish idiom," and the even more insulting strictures of Pierre Lasserre who detected in him a Germanic foreigner clumsily trying his hand at the French language and placed him beside the German romantics and, horror of horrors, Nietzsche. To Claudel, Scandinavia and Germany were the land of Luther, his constant *bête noire*. He was living in Tièntsin when he read the rapturous eulogies of Ibsen by his correspondent Suarès; like many an exile, he rose up in defense of the French heritage that to him, born inland and close to the Belgian frontier, was Mediterranean. He answered Suarès in revealing lines, on 5 February 1909:

> Ibsen inhabits a sunless country in which people never come out of their darkness. His is a theater of mutes, in which gestures rather than words make up the discourse. He is sinister, even more than he is tragic. In the fog, the action has no aim, people move about without our knowing what they are doing. What is lacking in those northern populations is passion, intensity. They do not react. . . . Those Kant, Ibsen, Schopenhauer, and I would add Tolstoy to them, live quietly and as bourgeois with deleterious ideas which are drugs which would dissolve, stupefy or convulse us, Latins. . . .

Claudel nurtured a lifelong grudge against Kant, whose works he never opened after his years at the lycée. The refutation of the traditional proofs of God's existence in the *Critique of Pure Reason* and, even more, the second *Critique* had infuriated him. He expressed himself even more perversely on Goethe, "the Philistine of Weimar," an "ass'" as he called him, a humorless pagan whom he was close to identifying with Mephistopheles. He enjoyed venting his scorn for Goethe (and, jointly, for Thomas Mann) at dinner parties, and it was after one such provocative demonstration, which angered his neighbor at an official table, Mrs. Agnes Meyer, that she and the French ambassador set up a lasting friendship. Obviously Claudel could not repress his fits of passionate anger; he depicted himself as Furiosus, a bad-tempered and irascible man, in his *Entretiens dans le Loir-et-Cher* and, cynically or humorously, he admitted to some of his confidents, and to himself, that he often hardly knew the works of the authors whom he summarily condemned to inferno. "It is so much better not to know what there is in the books which we talk about. It enables one to judge them sweepingly," he declared to Henri Guillemin, who reports it is in his book *Pas à pas*. In quite a few cases, Claudel's wrath was aimed at himself under the guise of foreign writers, at features that he well knew he had in common with them, or at his former self who had been fascinated by them. A case in point is that of Wagner. The change that came over Claudel's attitude toward Wagner, first ardently loved, probably the inspirer of the splendid love duet between Mesa and Ysé in the second act of *Partage de Midi,* then bitterly ridiculed in a long dialogue composed in 1926 in Tokyo and on other occasions, deserves a whole study in itself, and it would be a revealing one on Claudel's personality. As late as 1965 (1 April), when he could no longer vituperate and protest, Claudel was called, in the title of an article in the *London Times Literary Supplement,* "Wagner of letters"!

Being characterized as a Nietzschean, as he has repeatedly been since his death, would have angered Claudel even more. He vehemently asserted that he had never read much of Nietzsche and never opened his books without deep horror. One may be a Nietzschean without having read much of Nietzsche, of course. Through the literary circles with which Claudel was occasionally in touch when he was in Paris, around 1892–1900 (though probably not before the publication of his "Nietzschean" drama, *Tête d'or,* in 1889, the very same year that the German philosopher went mad), Claudel must have heard Nietzsche discussed. Repeatedly, however, he asserted that he had not been able to bear Nietzsche's lack of reasonableness and of logic, contrasting with Aristotle and St. Thomas into whom Claudel had steeped himself after his conversion. So he asserted to Jean Amrouche in the *Mémoires improvisés* (p. 90). Elsewhere, in an article aptly entitled "In the Face of the European Vertigo," given to *Le Figaro* in January 1939 (*Oeuvres en Prose,* Pléiade, p. 1139), he declared, in words that may be taken at their face value:

> I have many times tried to read the works of unhappy Nietzsche. But always, that debility of definitions, that is to say that lack of principles and consequently that contradictory chaos of deductions, that childish petulance, that violence born of weakness, those eruptions of individual and animal instinct replacing the serene light of general consideration, those haggard mutterings, those grimaces and invectives of a slave in revolt, filled me with horror and disgust; after a few pages, I could not pursue.

Those irate outbursts of Claudel against almost everything German were not merely what the French call *"boutades,"* the sallies of an impatient and vulnerable old man unwilling to put up with what threatens his faith as a total believer and to tolerate any conciliation with what he deems to be diabolical. They expressed the distrust and even the visceral repulsion of a Frenchman toward the Germanic world. The sight of Germany acclaiming Hitler and rushing headlong to war and chaos, on the eve of World War II, naturally confirmed Claudel in his political, and literary, nationalism. Like many of his compatriots, he saw Nazism, not just as an historical accident, but as "the fruit of a tradition which could be traced back to the Teutonic Knights"; beside it, however, and in contrast with it, he placed the tradition of the Holy Roman Empire and the dream of Leibniz, that of a federation in which the varied ethnic groups of the old Austria-Hungary should have coexisted in a livable equilibrium. In an interview he gave to Georges Cattaui that appeared on 20 May 1939 in *La Bourse égyptienne* (Cairo), he maintained, however, his stubborn aversion for German letters. Hölderlin, Novalis, the earlier German mystics left him cold:

> They believe that imagination should lead into the unreal, into the mist! never any clear images: none of those terms which, brought together from afar, are confronted. The same mental faculty which produces the syllogism is also that which makes the image. [But with the Germans] always that debility of definitions, those haggard whisperings. I hold all that is gaseous in horror: it is gloomy and dreary. Among them, Hoffmann is the one whom I prefer, and Heine who had wit, at least. . . . Those people, for me, are devoid of muscle, of virility. And that often holds true also for the poets of England and Ireland, that great befogged mystagogue of Yeats, for example. . . .

Claudel's distrust of "the northern fogs," as French nationalists like Jules Lemaître and Charles Maurras were then fond of calling them, his equal distrust of Tolstoy, "that exhibitionist," as he called him in 1911 in a letter to Suarès, and of all the Russian authors except Dostoevsky, hardly make him a meek follower of the French tradition as it was offered to French schoolboys by their nineteenth-century teachers. Foreigners generously attribute the gift of logic to the French; the French themselves prefer to view the compliment as a very dubious one. Among the very few lines of foreign verse that they like to make their own is the famous peremptory statement in which Walt Whitman asserts his right to contradict himself, as a proof of his containing multitudes. Before the American poet, Baudelaire had hinted that there lurks a uniquely voluptuous pleasure in blatantly contradicting oneself and even in betraying a cause once espoused. If ever Claudel's literary and artistic statements become collected in one volume (some of them have been in a book translated as *Claudel on the Theatre,* University of Miami Press, 1972), readers will be entertained by the succesive—at times even the nearly simultaneous—pros and cons, anathemas and eulogies uttered by that typical Frenchman in tones equally peremptory and self-assured. Our paltry critics' minds might be reassured if we could trace a clear evolution from one point of view to another, from romantic and rhetorical exaltation for instance to classical restraint, or from the pale and diembodied muses of the symbolist poets to the baroque sumptuousness of *Le Soulier de Satin*. But no such curve can, in all fairness, be suggested. Claudel confessed repeatedly to being a hot-tempered man, whose wrath had to boil over and spill invectives (especially at those who appeared to him as enemies of his faith). The purgation once effected, he recovered his balance and could turn if not into a model of charity, at least indifferent and almost lenient. One case of such contradiction among many is Claudel's attitude toward a fellow-diplomat and a fellow-dramatist, Giraudoux. In 1931, having heard in Washington about the play by Giraudoux on *Judith* that had been staged in Paris, the ambassador took up the cudgels in a letter to Darius Milhaud (19 November), calling it "stinking garbage" or something equivalent; on 16 December 1931, he had not yet soothed his anger and pictured Giraudoux in these terms: "He aptly represents the lecherous and Voltairian littérateur who is the controlling figure in our literature. It is easy to imagine the spruce and sour old man that he will be in a few years" (Giraudoux was Claudel's junior by fifteen years). Then in 1940, answering a question on literary trends for *Le Figaro littéraire*, the same Claudel praised "that quality of original poetical penetration which Giraudoux had brought into French literature" and which did honor to his country. In 1944, as Giraudoux had just died, he wrote a touching four-page farewell to him, lauding the grace and the elegance he had as a man and as an author. Not a word on *Judith*, although Claudel's instinct had not erred when he had detected in Giraudoux one of the most Voltairian Frenchmen (with more poetry in his soul than there had been in Voltaire) and a humansit totally impervious to the notion of original sin.

Claudel's injustice to his own French contemporaries is far from being an isolated phenomenon; a creator worthy of the name has to preserve his faith in the uniqueness of his message and of his manner. If he felt too warm an admiration for any of his fellow writers, or even if he understood any of them with too much sympathy, he would be afraid of undergoing their influence. At any cost, he must preserve his own originality, even if it entails nurturing his prejudices and proving blatantly unjust. Claudel was fully aware of it. A revealing sentence in his *Journal* (I, 553), obviously referring to himself, reads: "Do not ask him for his opinion on his fellow-writers, for he could only cease being unjust by ceasing also to be sincere." Moreover Claudel, like other converts, could not but feel that a Catholic poet like himself was surrounded by agnostics, pagans, hostile and Satanic authors in secular France (Gide, Valéry, Proust among the major figures) or, worse still, by Catholics (Péguy, Bremond, Bernanos, occasionally even Mauriac, Maritain, Massignon) with whom he sharply disagreed on theological matters of vital import to him. Catholics, indeed, had been for years his most relentless critics. Supporters of Catholicism were the members of the French Academy who, when the ambassador was already close to the venerable age of three score years and ten, slammed the door of the Academy on him, preferring pagans like Claude Farrère and Charles Maurras to him. Louis Aragon, a communist and long a surrealist, is the one contemporary writer on whom Claudel bestowed unstinted praise. He also eulogized Léger (St. John Perse), a fellow diplomat, a friend, and in some ways a disciple of his, in part for nonliterary reasons, and Francis Jammes, because Claudel had brought him within the fold of faith—perhaps emasculating his talent thereby.

Claudel's vituperations against most nineteenth-century French writers have been expressed so violently and so repeatedly, in his verse and in his prose essays, that we need not dwell on them here. The whole age was condemned by him as altogether un-Christian and as addicted to a joyless, bleak pessimism. He denounced Stendhal ferociously, and Michelet and Renan whose souls, if ever they had one, were now "with dead dogs" in hell. He could not help, however, admiring Michelet's prose, and he returned many times to the reading of Renan, as if to reassure himself that, as a writer of tepid and languid prose and as an infidel, Renan did deserve his contempt. A personal grudge lurked in that assault: the poet's sister had been an irreligious person who had admired and brought to her young brother Renan's *Life of Jesus*. Next to Rodin, whose mistress and disciple she had been, Renan appeared to Claudel as the influence most directly accountable for the madness into which she

sank for forty years. On Hugo, whom he resembled in more ways
than one and by whom he was obsessed all his life, Claudel con-
tradicted himself, shrewdly praising the novelist in him above the
poet. Sainte-Beuve was peremptorily dismissed as "the King of the
imbeciles" (November 1939). The Parnassians, the naturalists
fared even worse. To Paul Bourget, a self-appointed defender of the
faith, he reserved in 1893 a secure place in his inferno. Even to
Baudelaire and to Mallarmé, Claudel remained rather cool. He
seems to have been afraid to state the reasons for which he worshipped Rimbaud and remained reticent on the one poet who had
been the intercessor between him and God. His only fairly precise,
and highly penetrating, critical essay on a nineteenth-century poet
was the one he devoted to Verlaine, for whom his admiration never
flagged.

Did Claudel evince more affection for the earlier ages of French
literature, untainted as yet by Voltairian irony, by provocative atheism, or by the positivism of the nineteenth century, so abhorrent to
him? Very few are the French writers who are not secretly flattered
when they are lauded as classics and set beside their seventeenth-
century predecessors. Sartre placed himself as a dramatist in the Cornelian tradition and hailed Descartes as a forerunner of his own doctrine of freedom. Malraux, Camus enjoyed the *rapprochement* between Pascal and themselves that critics repeatedly sketched. Proust
harked back to Racine, Mme. de Sévigné, Saint-Simon. Claudel once
expressed some humorous satisfaction at having been ranked along-
side the classics.[1]

Here again however, Claudel reveals himself as deeply French in
the sense that he chose to be a dissenter, debunking the revered idols
of French professors, an anarchist, as he often called himself, who
had to curb his revolutionary individualism through finding a discipline in Catholic orthodoxy. On the age of the Renaissance, he very
seldom expressed himself, except to rejoice that it had also been the
age of the expansion of Christianity and of the Counter Reforma-
tion. He is one of the very few Frenchmen who have ever confessed
to a dislike of Montaigne; that Pascal could have been so strangely
fascinated by "a mind so light, so superficial and often plain silly"
(*Journal,* II, 144, May 1936) was to him distressive and reflected

unfavorably on Pascal. When in 1937 the weekly *Nouvelles littéraires* asked Claudel his opinion on the *Discours de la méthode,* then three centuries old, Claudel sent an arresting and solid article to demonstrate that Descartes was a poor writer (to whom not French, but Latin was a natural language), a loose reasoner lacking in rigor, and "a sort of Luther invoking freedom of conscience." On Pascal, a saint for many a French Catholic, Claudel varied; at the end of his life, he felt almost inclined to forgive him if, as Jacques Chevalier argued, one could trust the memoirs of an aged priest who received dying Pascal's confession and understood that Pascal had renounced his Jansenism. Until then, Claudel had proclaimed his hatred of the Jansenists, almost as repellent to him as the Protestants, and his distrust of Pascal. The subject of his denunciations of Pascal (and those of other anti-Pascalians, Gide, Valéry) deserves a whole volume. On the whole, Claudel's strictures are curiously close to those of the unbeliever Valéry. "Very soon," he declared to Henri Guillemin, "I sniffed a heretic in him. He is a fideist. He diminishes man, he stunts him. . . . He would want us to mutilate ourselves in order for us to be Catholics. But it is exactly the contrary. We must blossom forth, open ourselves." Pascal cannot be forgiven for having found the "infinite spaces" silent. "But they are not silent! they sing!" Valéry had likewise contrasted Pascal's famous phrase with the Psalmist's "Coeli enarrant gloriam Dei." However, Fénelon seemed to Claudel even more nefarious than Pascal, as nefarious as St. John of the Cross and those French mystics whom Abbé Bremond was tirelessly rediscovering and, in Claudel's judgment, foolishly overpraising. The mystics, even more than the pagans, were upbraided as his personal enemies.

Corneille was, along with Pascal, his pet hatred among the French classics. *Polyeucte,* exalted by Péguy (whom Claudel held in scant esteem) as a Christian masterpiece, aroused his laughter and his scorn. Talking to Mondor, to Cattaui, to Guillemin, he delighted in belittling him: "a repellent figure," "a clever lawyer devoid of poetic genius," a provincial bourgeois altogether closed to humility and charity, a fanatic of pride. His one redeeming grace was his bent toward heroism, absent from Shakespeare's theater. But "Corneille is nothing but pagan ethics, made even worse by Spanish bombast. All in him is false, theatrical, strained, verging on the ridiculous through being exaggerated, complicated, artificial . . ." (*Journal,* II, 283, September 1939). The worst of it was that he had been a pupil of the Jesuits, and the Jesuits, later, adopted and praised his plays, taught them to the men of the eighteenth century and of the Revolution, and infected them with that poison. "There is nothing like the Humanities to destroy humanity. The whole Cornelian theater goes against humanity (or mankind). Through Corneille and Seneca, the Jesuits poisoned generations of students. They thereby deserved to see their order dissolved under Clement XIV" (Text written in 1944 after the fiftieth performance of *Le Soulier de Satin*).

On Molière, Claudel, who prided himself on his sense of the comic, seldom expressed his views; he praised his gifts as a prose-writer, terse, muscular, quick and, more surprisingly, declared him a great lyric poet, the master of a lyricism that takes elements from reality and transmutes them into wit. But he added: "I can never forgive him *Le Misanthrope,* any more than I can forgive Corneille for *Polyeucte.*" Among the seventeenth-century classics, he preferred Bossuet (as a theologian, as the denouncer of "the variations of the Protestant churches," and especially as a supreme artist of prose) and Boileau (Texts respectively of 1927 and 1911, included in *Oeuvres en Prose,* Pléiade, pp. 437–38). Obviously, Claudel enjoyed iconoclastic paradoxes and flinging brutal anathemas at what the French professors held most dear. They had branded him as "un-French," and he was wreaking his revenge. A Jesuit, Father de Tonquédec, had upbraided him for being too remote from the Frenchmen of the seventeenth century; Claudel could neither disregard nor forgive such foolish lack of insight. He trampled upon their idols—most of them (Pascal and Bossuet excepted) pagan idols, as he remarked: "Classical literature is the result of an attempt, begun in the sixteenth century, to create a fictitious world into which Revelation never entered" (*Journal,* I, 1932). One of the favorite Racinian tragedies of the French academics was *Bérénice,* traditionally exalted for the simplicity of its plot and the poetical purity of its verse. Claudel, in February 1935 (*Journal,* II, 80–81), attended a performance of the play at the Théâtre français and jotted down: "crushing boredom. That sentimental marivaudage, that inexhaust-

ible casuistry on love, is what I most detest in French literature. . . .
It is distinguished and overwhelmingly dull . . . and to think that
Racine is made the foundation of the literary education of our poor
children."

At the very same time as Claudel was vituperating against those
sacred cows of the French, their seventeenth-century writers, often
called by them the masterpieces of "the Age of Reason," he was de-
fending those very same virtues of order, moderation, wisdom, and
even of reason. In a lecture delivered on 14 November 1927 in
Baltimore, on the relationship between poetry and religion (*Oeuvres
en Prose,* Pléiade, p. 58), the ambassador peremptorily asserted
(standing close to Poe's grave, as he remarked):

> Reason is good. Imagination is good. Sensitivity is good. Only
> heretics, or Jansenists like Pascal, may believe that any faculty of
> that human mind which God created, is in itself bad. Only dis-
> order and excess are bad.

Fifteen years earlier (1912), while still unacknowledged in his
own country and viewed with awe and horror as the foe of "French
clarity" and of artistic control, Claudel had publicly proclaimed:
"The principle of great art is an absolute avoidance of anything
unnecessary." That was not an isolated utterance designed to be-
wilder his denigrators. In 1910, in a reply to a newspaper then advocating neoclassical values, Claudel sent a fifteen line statement,[2]
praising classical discipline and summing it up in the lapidary pre-
cept that the French took over from the Greek and the Latin
tongues: "Rien de trop." He added:

> The safest thing which may be said about beauty is that it rests,
> above all, in a just composition and that the sense of measure, ir-
> reducible to scholastic formulas, is the crowning of those gifts of
> the artist, without which all other gifts are of no avail. Taste is
> another French word for wisdom. Classical art begins where the
> artist takes more interest in his work than in himself.

Gide, after he and Claudel had parted ways and were privately
jotting down in their journals scornful remarks on each other, sarcastically recalled how, at the beginnings of his literary career, Clau-

del had paraded his motto: "Nothing in excess." Had he lived by it? Not in Gide's opinion. But Claudel had grown equally scornful of Gide's alleged classicism, which, in the writings of his old age, was merely a screen for desiccation of sensibility and paralysis of imagination.

On one subject those two authors agreed: their literary beginnings had taken place in the heyday of symbolism; both had ventured for many years into several foreign literatures, conceived a passionate admiration for Dostoevsky, and been enthusiasts of Shakespeare. But they had learned to relish the qualities of their own national literature all the more through having explored others. Both, throughout their careers, indulged in the French game of tracing a literary parallel between Racine and Shakespeare. Both ended by offering reservations to their cult of Shakespeare and raising Racine to a pinnacle. In his long and very elaborate 1925 essay "Réflexions et propositions sur le vers français," Claudel had hailed the *Aeneid* and Racine's *Britannicus* as "masterpieces of the human spirit." The play *Bérénice,* which he had maligned elsewhere, was praised by him in 1934, as he commented in *Le Figaro* on his own drama *L'Otage,* the most "classical" of his plays, as representative of something deeply French—an insistence on the values of design, continuity, dignity, an ingenious counterpoint in which individual passions are "the clarification of a universal crisis or conflict of ideas." Later still, in 1954, the aging poet, at last successful on the stage, wrote for J. L. Barrault a conversation on Racine. The dialogue is between Claudel himself and an imaginary confident, Arcas, whose role is to elicit the vehement explosions of the poet. Shakespeare is in no way belittled. Claudel does not disavow the enthusiasm that *Hamlet* and *Macbeth* had once aroused in him. Still, Racine is the one who enraptures him. "Not a single beautiful feminine part in Shakespeare," asserts Arcas. Racine's lucidity and mastery in the delineation of evil progressively capturing Nero's soul are set above the unexplained and inexplicable changes from virtue to crime in the characters in *Macbeth.* Not one superfluous image, not one unnecessary line in Agrippine's long speech to her son in the fourth act of *Britannicus.* Even the Alexandrine line, once harshly mocked by Claudel as monotonous and symbolic of the French passion for thrift and for security, is declared to be admirable in Racine. "The pleasure which Racine gives is the intimate accord between thought and feeling; both multiply, one by the other, their thrill of delight to the point of ecstasy." Nothing more intelligently admiring has been written on Racine in our century, and Claudel does not endeavor to depict Racine as a Catholic as opposed to stoic, humanistic Corneille or to dark, pagan Shakespeare. He envisages him primarily as a poet.

His strictures on Shakespeare became harsher as he grew older and more attached to his native province and to his literary tradition. Some of them rested on differences of taste, aesthetic and moral. One play by Shakespeare revolted him in particular, *Romeo and Juliet,* perhaps because analogies could be traced between his own *Partage de Midi* and that love duet in Elizabethan style. As he was growing to ridicule Wagner's *Tristan,* which he had once loved overmuch, in the same 1927 *rêverie* on the German composer, Claudel expressed his revulsion at the "abominable jargon" and the artificial and pretentious style of the play; elsewhere, corresponding with J. L. Barrault, he declared it "hollow and noisy." Only *Measure for Measure* aroused in him a similar disgust, which he shared in this case with several English admirers of Shakespeare, Coleridge included. But the pessimism of Shakespeare's tragedies, the apparent revelling in the absurd of the characters in *Macbeth* and *King Lear* drew Claudel's pitiless condemnation. He did not, unlike many a commentator, speculate on Shakespeare's own religion, or lack of it, or identify the splendid rhetorical outbursts on "the tale told by an idiot" with the dramatist's own philosophy, of which we know nothing. Like not a few English or American readers of Shakespeare,[3] he was struck by the total lack of Christian charity or of Hellenic or Aeschylean moral message in the greatest of the tragedies. After attending a performance of *Lear* in Paris in November 1946 and formulating some shrewd observations on the staging and the acting of that nearly unstageable drama, Claudel added a few grave paragraphs on the substance of the tragedy:

> The Middle Ages are not far remote. Yet faith has disappeared from Shakespeare's theater as completely as if the Gospel had

never been preached to men. Paradise is lost. . . . Not a ray of
Christianity illuminates those desperate abysses of darkness.

He conjures up the monstrousness of the two elder daughters,
those members of the same families all in arms against each other,
the mad King at last finding Cordelia, in vain, since all he shakes in
his arms is that poor dying puppet. Shakespeare, Claudel concludes,
"never found God."

The same year (1946), Claudel, almost then an octogenarian,
was at last received at the French Academy, where he was to occupy
(he liked to recall it) the "seat" which had once been that of Racine. He was succeeding the critic Louis Gillet, who had written
good books of intelligent popularization on art, on Dante, and on
Shakespeare. Claudel seized the opportunity to tell again of his admiration for Dante's Christian poetry and to contrast Shakespeare
with him:

> When Shakespeare begins to write, a catastrophe has taken place,
> the shadow of which extends over the whole of the English litera-
> ture that followed it, comparable to that wild valley mentioned by
> the Psalmist, in which the Puritan Bunyan and many a pilgrim
> without a compass will be trudging along. Paradise has been lost,
> the paradise of Faith. In vain do Shakespeare's heroes, male and
> female, ask each other for it with all the resources of poetry, of
> passion and of despair. . . .

Elsewhere, as if he had been intent upon renouncing his young
man's fascination with the English dramatist to which he had been
proud to be compared, aged Claudel returned to his reasons for preferring Racine, or the Greek dramatists, to Shakespeare. The gaping
lack in Shakespeare's world was, he maintained,

> . . . . the most important half, heaven, the third dimension, the
> vertical direction. We are entertained, interested, fascinated, but
> never does Shakespeare take hold of us, grasp us by the throat,
> confront us with a pitiless sphinx, as, for example, Antigone, Cas-
> sandra, Alcestis do to us. . . . All those characters go about their
> business, obeying their own weight. Never are they led or forced
> to transcend themselves. What do I have in common with them?

We are almost embarrassed to have to whisper to ourselves Hamlet's very words: "Man delights me not, nor woman either."[4]

French history is too long, the French literary heritage is too rich for any Frenchman to accept the whole of it unreservedly. In every one of them, there lurks an anarchist who coexists with a conservative, a Jacobin who would gladly guillotine his adversaries, or relegate them to that hell where Claudel, holding crêpes suzette with a long fork over green and red fragrant flames, jocularly hoped Gide was burning. Few members of that allegedly Cartesian nation have ever equated logic with consistency or reasonableness, or agreeing to disagree with their rationalism. Claudel rejected many things French but never felt at home in Britain, Germany, America. The most obstinate commentator on the Old Testament of all the modern French, and of all French writers, he rarely set foot in the land where the Prophets of Israel and Christ had lived. A Catholic convinced that no salvation was possible outside the Roman orthodoxy, he reserved his deepest affection for only two foreign nations, China and Japan. Branded by many of his countrymen as a revolutionary iconoclast and a gravedigger of the venerable French language, he is now acknowledged to have been, of all twentieth-century writers, the one closest to Racine, and even to Balzac and to Hugo, in the typical manner of the French romantics who turn out to have been classical writers under a cloak of rhetorical violence, working for the ultimate triumph of the national values that they questioned.

"Claudel and the French Literary Tradition" has been published in *The France of Claudel,* Special ed. Henri Peyre, *Review of National Literatures,* 4, No. 2 (Fall 1973), pp. 11–33.

## NOTES

1. In a letter to me after the publication of my article "Le Classicisme de Claudel" in *La Nouvelle Revue française,* September 1932. The article is reprinted in *Claudel: les critiques de notre temps* (Garnier, 1970).
2. It is reproduced in my volume *Qu'est-ce que le classicisme?* (Paris: Nizet, 1965), p. 252.
3. Among them the philosopher Clement Webb, in *Pascal's Philosophy of Religion,* p. 94 ("Shakespeare, of whom one is tempted to say that the

Christian religion is the one thing he did not understand"); Sir H.J.C. Grierson in *Cross Currents in English Literature of the XVIIth Century* (London: Chatto and Windus, 1929); George Santayana, "The Absence of Religion in Shakespeare" in *Interpretations of Poetry and Religion* (New York: Charles Scribner's Sons, 1900); and a number of American scholars who refuted Wilson Knight's endeavors to see the sacrifice of Christ as everywhere present in Shakespeare's plays.

4. I quoted the passage, to be found in Jean Claude Berton's *Shakespeare and Claudel* (La Palatine, 1958), in "Shakespeare and Modern French Criticism," *The Persistence of Shakespeare, Idolatry* (Detroit: Wayne State University Press, 1964).

# 6. Is Literature Dead?
## Or Dying?

THE QUESTION IS NOT JUST A RHETORICAL ONE, which might provide a provoking title for an essay. It should not just serve as a convenient pretext for an older man to vent his distrust of younger writers and critics, by whom he might instinctively feel threatened. It has been asked of others and myself repeatedly and earnestly in the last few years by young and old alike, by scientists, sociologists, doctors, lawyers, bankers, professional women, housewives, and ladies of leisure, who all would like to read engrossing novels, serious or playful, in their spare hours and during their vacations. A growing number of them are sadly disappointed by the volumes that book clubs send them. They feel bitter at the reviewers who, in weeklies and monthlies, have persuaded them to purchase volumes that bore them, puzzle them, or disgust them. They may be seen in public libraries, in bookstores, questioning the persons in charge or even each other, ransacking the shelves in search of a contemporary work of imaginative literature that might afford them pleasure and intellectual excitement and justify the disbursement of the eight or ten dollars now asked for almost any new book in hard covers. Not a few of them, generously, or masochistically, inclined to distrust their own American culture, ask me to point out French volumes that might entertain or enrich them, as Proust, Mauriac, Saint-Exupéry, Colette did when they were in college. Bravely, they attempt the latest of the *nouveaux romans,* only to find their patience defeated after a hundred pages and to nod their heads mournfully at what has happened to Gaullist or post-Gaullist France. As a last resort, and nostalgically, they reopen their old copies of Anatole France or of Zola, or they resort to English stories with a spiced up Victorian flavor, *The French Lieutenant's Woman* or *G,* by skilled renovators of last century's models. In despair, or in resignation, reading clubs, and even couples who insist upon some evening literary perusing as a relief from the television commercials, decide to read aloud to each other *Jane Eyre, Middlemarch,* or the complete works of Trollope. What incitement to read will young generations carry away from college with them, whose taste has been "refined" by *The Catcher in the Rye,* Updike's *Couples,* or Roth's *The Breast* and whose extracurricular excitement has been provided by Miller's *Sexus* or by Burroughs' *Naked Lunch?* Are the dire prophecies of Marshall McLuhan coming true, and is imaginative literature gloomily breathing its last gasp?

The question is here being echoed, and hopefully answered more in distress than in anger, by one who never was a professional pessimist or an obstinate mourner for the so-called good old days. On the contrary, his ambition was, and still is, to stand up for the moderns and to encourage young writers to create a tradition, rather than to follow, or to accept without questioning them, the conventions and the assumptions of an earlier era. He decided, years ago, to devote his life to the teaching and interpretation of literature and the arts because he saw in them the greatest source of enjoyment accessible to people living in a technological civilization. His ambition was to develop in his students and readers that sense of the past which may endow them with historical imagination and enable them not to remain merely the citizens of one age and of one country. If he stressed occasionally the relevance of apparent irrelevance and the modernity of the past, he also agreed that a teacher could not altogether ignore the demand for relevance and that he might, without loss of caste, take a vital interest in the immediacy of the present. His contention, and that of many students of contemporary literature, was always that, if interpreted with warmth and with some involvement in the issues of today, fine arts, and literature even more so, because it is better able to convey ideas, afford an insight into the present hardly matched by other studies. Imaginative literary works dramatize our inner conflicts, intensify life, and enhance our understanding of the world without us as well as of the world within. A Frenchman himself, he acquiesced early in the view proudly held by his countrymen that literature may also be prophecy. The expression of acutely sensitive natures, often dreaming of the future as a compensation for a dreary present or as a means of escape from their anguish as artistic and individualistic beings, literature foresees what is to come and often helps bring it about. It has repeatedly been remarked that a compatriot of the eighteenth-century *philosophes* and of Balzac, naturally, if arrogantly, views his role in the light of those precursors of the Revolution of 1789 who were lauded or blamed for the distorted application that was made of their doctrines. As for Balzac, whom Baudelaire was the first to call a visionary far removed from the copying of life, or as for Hugo, Michelet, Rimbaud, it has become a commonplace of criticism to assert that they depicted, long in advance, the age that succeeded them and that they heralded, not the one in which they wrote. The lofty claim made for literature by those who deeply believe in it and read its modern productions with serious attention is that it not only foresees what is to come, it also helps create it or orientate it. Thus it may answer Rimbaud's famous cry: "Change life!"

The contemplation of the present low estate of literature in several countries of the West is distressing for him who set such faith in it and lived by it. To be sure, the critic thus inclined to grumble and to lament must first be suspicious of his own judgment, since he has probably lost much freshness as he has grown old and he may well suffer from a lack of flexibility. His view of the present may also be warped by a long acquaintance with the classics, in whom he was once nurtured, and by his familiarity with the masterpieces of the past, which have been elucidated over and over again by commentators. Still, a little common sense warns him that the brief present, by which two dozen years are usually implied, is not to be unfairly compared with "classical music" or with the painting, the poetry, and the fiction of two or three hundred years. The so-called modern, or rather contemporary, production can only be set, in all fairness, against other spans of twenty-five years in the past.

Other safeguards should be erected against any ill-tempered condemnation of one's own age; it may well be that several of the works that will, one day, be singled out as the most profound, and even as the most representative, of our time are either unknown to a contemporary observer or remain ignored by him. Some may still be in manuscript form (as Rimbaud's or Gerard Manley Hopkins' poems were during their lifetime); others are memoirs or novels that may appear only posthumously, or that have only been published in little known magazines or in limited and scarce editions. Besides, we are all fallible, and those of us whose interest lies in the productions of their own time are often the least impartial. Most French critics and many a novelist were put off by Proust's novel around 1919–25 and repeated the silly quip of an English wit that his success with a coterie would prove no more lasting than a hairdresser's "Marcel wave." A. E. Housman advised against venturing a translation of Proust into English. The most famous writers of the early twenties, nonacademic as well as college dons, failed to see much, if anything, in Kafka, in *Ulysses,* in D. H. Lawrence's best stories, and even in *The Waste Land.* I have elsewhere (in *The Failures of Criticism,* 1944) studied many cases of such misunderstanding between writers and contemporary critics and quoted Wordsworth's pronouncement (in 1815) as the shrewdest statement on that eternal and universal feud: "Every author, as far as he is great and at the same time original, has had the task of creating the taste by which he is to be enjoyed." No one has ever satisfactorily defined "greatness" in the realm of literature or of art, but one thing about it appears certain. Greatness is not; it becomes. As in science, the fecundity of an idea, of a hypothesis, of a new technique and the wealth of varied echoes that a work may arouse testify to the lasting power, hence also the greatness, of a literary work. No one literally could, while those writers were alive, have surmised what progeny Flaubert, Mallarmé, Lawrence, or Kafka would enjoy or produce nor foreseen the future avalanche of ingenious commentaries that has not yet quite succeeded in stifling "The Afternoon of a Faun," *Women in Love,* or *The Trial.*

All those warnings and others being duly borne in mind, many an observer of the literary scene between 1950 and 1972 feels dejected by what confronts him. Like all contemporaries, and in particular like many professors, he is tempted to complain that there are too few signposts to guide him: no clear trend, no neatly defined movement, no geographic or ideological group, no young talents rallying behind a mentor or a technical innovator. Historians may some day discover among us the equivalent of the Southern Agrarians, of the imagists, of the social critics or of the conservatives of the 1930's; but such artificial classifications have little reality and offer mere mnemotechnic advantages to the writer of textbooks. Confusion there is around us, and there always has been: that should act as a challenge to the courageous observer. All groups, all trends have only been worth what the individual's talent was worth. All criticism should ultimately distrust generalizations and labels and come down to an evaluation of the personal achievement of those creators who have enlightened us and moved us.

The American scene since 1950 has witnessed a number of promising starts, but it now seems strewn with failures, or at least with sadly unfulfilled promises. Gone is the age when, while the country was in the throes of the Depression and obstinately isolating itself from foreign entanglements, between 1929 and 1939, its literature provided Europe with splendid excitement and won the admiration of otherwise hypercritical French minds like Gide, Malraux, Sartre, Camus, and Mme. Claude-Edmonde-Magny. The United States is still the western country with the richest variety of talents and the most dynamic, at times the most hysterical, literary activity. Yet, there also literature as we have known it seems moribund, and not a single name has arisen, in fiction, to match what Fitzgerald, Hemingway, Faulkner, even Dos Passos at his best and Steinbeck at his most earnest or at his most humorous represented before World War II. Much was expected for a time from authors who had written the most ambitious books of the war of 1941-45, while that same war appeared to have daunted the efforts of the European novelists; but George Horne Burns died prematurely, Norman Mailer shifted his energies elsewhere, Irwin Shaw failed to recapture the gifts that had, in his *Young Lions,* aroused much hope. The best of their successors, Robert Penn Warren and Saul Bellow, have proved uneven; one may doubt that a single novel by either will survive among the classics of this midcentury. *Herzog* and *Mr. Sammler's Planet* have been grossly overpraised by reviewers, while the author, one of the most acute critical minds among American writers, deserved a better challenge. William Styron is not yet fifty and may still assume the outstanding if solitary role of the most daring and forceful novelist of his generation; he had, in *Lie Down in Darkness,* the unorganized and uncontrolled power of a new Thomas Wolfe and, subsequently, a visionary imagination and an insight into hatred and violence that struck many of us as worthy of Faulkner. How slow, however, seems the process of maturing in the very best writers of fiction of that age group, and how monotonous their obsession with drunkenness, sex, impotence, and madness!

More disappointing has been the stubborn refusal to grow of a dozen other writers whose talent first dawned in the decade following Pearl Harbor: Nelson Algren, Vance Bourjaily, Frederick Buchner, Paul Bowles, Merle Miller, William Goyen, Truman Capote. The beat generation spent its vigor recklessly in adolescent onslaughts against most intellectual attitudes and against any normal emotion. The rejection of all mental and artistic discipline doomed Jack Kerouac's stories, and the even more elementary and conventional ones of the Irish-American J. P. Donleavy, to a cheap form of romanticism. James Jones, after an early and ephemeral success, overwhelmed and wrecked any good will among potential readers with the monstrous 1250 pages of *Some Came Running.* He needed the kind of adviser and editor that Thomas Wolfe had once been fortunate to find to prune his ridiculously overstuffed and awkward narrative. Must every American novel offer us the same dismal sight of drunks, rapists, and prostitutes, whose psychology is never even probed and whose behavior is never raised to epic stature? Must we smile with condescension at such old-fashioned criteria for literary enjoyment as were formulated by George Eliot, reviewing German novels of peasant life in the *Westminister Review* in 1856: "The greatest benefit we owe to the artist, whether painter, poet or novelist, is the extension of our sympathies"?

Yet some of those novelists are men of culture, with a perspective on other literatures than their own and a mastery of style that often reaches brilliance. John Updike is one of them; hardly out of Harvard, he wrote entertaining and humorous poetry and intellectual critical reviews. He saw through the skilled and detached artificiality of Borges and Nabokov's even colder, soulless virtuoso mastery over words. But he somehow failed to endow books like *The Centaur, The Farm,* and *Bech* with any density or any credibility. *Rabbit Run* and even more the gloomy artificial symbolism of *Rabbit Redux* hardly rise above the average, and now old-fashioned, naturalist novel. *Couples* attempted to be more entertaining and more frankly satirical; it hardly eschewed monotony, however, and the language as well as the personality of those mechanical fornicators in suburbia betrayed a dismal view of American promiscuous love without joy and without tears that could be that of a Puritan moralist. Bernard Malamud is no less gifted, with a keen sense for the grotesque and a sociological eagerness to study American Jews and their self-centered lives. But *The Assistant,* the looser and more comical misadventures of a Jewish professor in *A New Life,* and the short stories, where Malamud's ambition is better attuned to his limited talent, somehow do not raise their author, a competent craftsman, to the level of last-ingly impressive fiction. Philip Roth, among the Jewish novelists, has had more impact upon the public attention. He is indeed a superb storyteller, ironical, hilarious, savagely corrosive—Portnoy may well remain a type almost as popular as Sinclair Lewis' Babbitt, and his two-dimensional mother rises to a Dickensian comic stature. Still, one wishes he would attempt a more ambitious theme and take his talent more seriously. Success may well have spoiled him too soon. He, like John Cheever and J. D. Salinger, appears to be more at home in the short story, neatly rounded off but content with stay-ing on the surface of life, than in the creation of fictional characters gradually revealed or in the arranging of significant episodes laid in varied surroundings.

Others have attempted to revive the fable and have indulged a taste for parables and semiallegorical stories. John Barth is probably the most cultured and the most ambitious of those genteel and professional novelists, but it is doubtful that the representative novel of our age will be one of those stilted and self-conscious variations on a mythological theme. The ambition to handle big, and often abstract, subjects has, since 1950 or so, been the noble goal of American writers of fiction (Styron in *Nat Turner,* Vance Bourjaily in *The Hound of Earth,* Katherine Anne Porter in *Ship of Fools,*

John Hawkes in his deliberately unreal stories, *The Cannibal,* or *Second Skin*). The mastery of luxuriant language and a Flaubertian concern for style have been among the virtues of several of those writers courted by English departments throughout the country. But the power to handle huge themes and to impart a sense of imaginative recreation of life through their style, or perhaps in spite of it, fails those artists.

If there seems to be a dearth of powerful conquest of exterior or of inner reality in today's fiction in the United States, those readers who have traditionally preferred to turn to the novel of Britain find little comfort. After some superciliousness and condescending sulking at what they had long regarded as American vulgarity and formlessness, the English critics have lately consented to bow before what they have called "American imagination." Well might they. None of the successors to Joyce and Lawrence, not even Graham Greene or Malcolm Lowry, the most visionary talents of the last thirty years, has filled the void left in British letters. English critics themselves have felt not a little embarrassed when, repeatedly asked which of their writers could be nominated, along with Americans, Germans, French or Russian authors, for the Nobel Prize, they have had to fall back on long faded E. M. Forster, or on Joyce Cary or Angus Wilson. The impact of their fiction on the continent or on other English-speaking lands has been minimal since World War II; and Lord Snow, with his papery creatures wrestling with the quandaries of scientists in and out of love, his wife (a better storyteller than he), or that Oxford philosopher attracted to complicated stories of sordidness and crime, Iris Murdoch, the most tirelessly inventive novelist of today's Britain, have not restored the English novel to the preeminence that it long enjoyed unchallenged. Nor has English poetry, since the brilliant debuts of Auden, Spender, MacNeice, and Day Lewis in the 1930's, risen to the challenge that both the English poetical tradition and the time of stress and of self-doubts lived by Britain might have offered it.

The bitterest disappointment of all is the one that confronts the observer of today's French literature (1950-72), when he bears in mind the achievement of the first post-war era, that of 1919-39. There is hardly any literary review today wielding any influence or primarily concerned with literature. The *Revue de Paris,* the *Mercure de France,* the *Revue hebdomadaire,* the *Revue bleue,* the *Revue Universelle,* and a dozen others have all perished. *Les Temps modernes* has, for all practical purposes, banished literature from its concern. *La Nouvelle Revue française* has failed to reveal a single new talent in a decade. The leftist *Europe* devotes well-informed and eclectic numbers to writers of the past, from Michelet and Nerval to Proust and Éluard, but lays no claim to any scouting for young writers of promise. *Tel Quel* and *Change,* and a few specialized journals by academics, seem to have taken it to heart to repel the common reader and to stifle any desire for aesthetic enjoyment in him under pseudoscientific discussions of abstruse problems of technique. In this reader's opinion, their solemn pontiffs (Sollers, Ricardou, Faye) have proved unable or unwilling to write a single readable work of fiction and have substituted for critical appraisal of books by their contemporaries what the French call "terrorism in literature"—the denouncing as reactionaries of all those who refuse to agree with their vituperations.

At one time in the 1920's, it was possible to enjoy simultaneously novels by Gide, Mauriac, Green, Cocteau, Aragon, Duhamel, Romains, Giono, and a dozen others. Then, soon after, one could hail a new generation of novelists of tragic or epic power (Bernanos, Malraux, Saint-Exupéry, Guilloux) and of poets of the magnitude of Breton, Éluard, Reverdy, Char, Desnos ready to replace their still productive elders: Claudel, Valéry, St. John Perse, Supervielle, Max Jacob. Poetry has not died since then, but it hardly ever reaches the public. The new novelists, their novelty already faded, their technical tricks stale, are invited to lecture in Nordic countries and in the United States; they do not conceal the fact that American teachers, in their eagerness to keep up with the latest Parisian fashions, are their best, almost their sole, customers. Not one of their novels has done well in translation, and American publishers voice their bitterness at having rashly listened to a few teachers claiming to stand at the "avant-garde." After the failure of the public to respond to the latest, the well-nigh unreadable, antinovels by Robbe-Grillet, Nathalie Sarraute, Michel Butor, not to mention the more disastrous misfits by Sollers, Faye, or Le Clézio, publishers are growing wary. They balk, with some reason, at the 500 or 600 page novels on which the French have lately bestowed their year-end prizes: *Le Sac du Palais d'Eté* by Pierre-J. Rémy, *Les Bêtises* by Jacques Laurent, *La Gloire de l'Empire* by Jean d'Ormesson, all exotic or utopian stories, replete with essaylike digressions, by highly sophisticated and overlearned intellectuals whose most sedulous care appears to be to make it clear that they are not taken in by the stories they are relating. Intellectual lucidity and sophistication are present in abundance, but the condescending tone of the skeptical author (who can hardly be called a storyteller, since he does his very best to avoid telling a story) refrigerates the reader of good will. An earlier Goncourt prize novel, *Le Roi des Aulnes* by Michel Tournier, found a publisher and a translator and appeared late in 1972 as *The Ogre*. It had been extolled by hyperbolic Parisian reviewers as the revelation of a first creator. Twelve months later, it had sunk into oblivion.

Sartre, Camus, and Malraux began to pall upon the reading public after the acclaim that, around the war years, had raised them to a pinnacle. Their message, their symbolism, probably even their technique reflected or suited their own era, and it was only natural for another generation to attempt a different kind of literature, voicing their own yearnings. It has been fortunate for Sartre and for Camus that *Nausea* or *The Stranger* discouraged disciples and imitators. But young generations, indifferent to the cold, virtuoso feats of technique of the "new" novelists, are seized by a strange nostalgia for the days when the existentialist authors evinced some concern for social and political issues, attempted to provide the lineaments of a faith in freedom and in responsibility, and called themselves the new humanists. Metaphysical issues and concern for the underprivileged classes are apparently no fit subjects for the "new" novelists, several of them of Marxist allegiance and all of them self-proclaimed foes of "the Establishment." Their primary anxiety is "to contest language," as they put it, and often to condemn it, advocating the virtue of silence through three hundred thousand words. Their elaborate works, ranging back and forth through time, skilled at puzzling the reader, often at imprisoning him in a cage within which he spins aimlessly, are structured after a fashion. They appear to be addressed to other fellow technicians and to ingenious critics, but not to the public. The latter is not even insulted, and thus challenged, as the middle class was when Balzac and Flaubert upbraided it and caricatured it. It is ignored. The sections of these puzzle novels are elaborately contrived to fit into each other eventually. But any relation they might have with life itself is left out. The only questions obsessively asked by the novelists concern their own creative process and the suspicion in which they hold their medium. Their wailing is never spent on their characters, to whom they deny all coherence, or even a semblance of existence, but on the novelist's inability ever to know any mind other than his own. These self-styled revolutionaries are content to begin and to end their revolt with language.

What are the underlying reasons that may account for the poverty and the sterility of present-day literature? There are more educated Americans and Frenchmen living today than at any other time in history. Those of us who have had, for the last forty years, students as captive audiences are prompt to assert that the young people of these last two decades have been as keen, as earnest, as imaginative, and as divided against themselves as their predecessors were in the thirties. But they do not choose writing as a vocation. They are obviously drawn to science, to social and psychological studies, to law, to administration, even to journalism. There have been periods in history in which the professions of administration and the pursuit of business lured the majority of the promising members of an age group. France lived through such an era under Napoleon the First; literature suffered from sterility, and the three or four outstanding talents all came from Switzerland. France enjoyed, during the Second Empire, a wave of prosperity and of industrial growth, just as she is doing at the present time, with a predominance of material values and a sharply rising standard of living. But the reign of Napoleon the Third seems, to many of us, the time when a courageous literature of protest, advocating the purity of art and the loftiness of the writer's profession, flourished; the Parnassians, Baudelaire, Flaubert, Taine, Renan were the mouthpieces of that age's aspirations. The impressionist painters as well as Verlaine and Mallarmé discovered and asserted their artistic vocation in opposition to the forces that then threatened to throttle literature. The counterculture of today, in contrast, cuts a sorry figure.

The competition of the mass media, and especially (where the French scene is concerned) of the cinema, has also been responsible for robbing literature of some of its potential talents. Oral absorption of knowledge has, for many of the young, replaced the bookish culture of earlier generations. The primacy of the book may well be imperiled, and the reluctance of many teenagers to perceive, in the legacy of the past, any relevance to their quandary has contributed to their inability to discriminate among ephemeral works and to select those that might become classics. Even in countries of Western Europe where the eagerness of Marshall McLuhan to abdicate before the new Moloch has not been generally imitated, ominous warnings have been uttered about the declining number of persons who care to purchase books. Fewer and fewer youngsters out of college dream nowadays of beginning their career with a tragedy, a volume of romantic verse, or a semiautobiographical novel, as their grandfathers had done. They look to the movies or to television scripts as an outlet for their creative urges. In American schools, where the choice of the books to be read by the young is often left to the teacher or to the principal, anything smacking of literature is being displaced in favor of the most elementary, and often of the most coarsely written, biographies or books of protest against the culture of the so-called Establishment. Teenagers, to be sure, have to be weaned from sugary, girlish stories and Christmas fairy tales, but the poverty of style and of content of the reading to which they are being exposed is not likely to polish their literary taste, nor to provide them with much insight into their fellow men.

It would be idle to mourn the gradual loss of the former privileges of literature and to lament what the written word must today concede to the audio-visual media. The follies of the Dreyfus case, of the Boer war, of Hitlerism were, after all, perpetrated by generations that had, presumably, been fed on Victorian fiction, on sentimental French and *gemuetlich* German novels. No one will grudge the young their tapping new sources of pleasure. But it is sad to observe that literature itself has lacked the vitality to respond victoriously to the challenge of the mass media. Painting a century ago knew how to gain from the development of photography, which enabled it to discard the imitation of reality. The theater likewise gained from the rivalry of the movies and concentrated on what it could achieve better than the screen. Poets discovered a new type of symbolist beauty after renouncing descriptive, narrative, and didactic poetry. Fiction today should differentiate itself from journalism and from the sociological essay, if need be through absorbing the best in them. Too often, it has chosen instead to be defeatist. Its practitioners confess to being baffled by the complexity of the contemporary scene. They take refuge in a world of childish fantasy that has little of the freshness and acuteness of a child's perception.

Neither the circumstances nor the political climate around us, nor even the mass media are to blame, but the writers themselves. Some of them (Kingsley Amis or John Wain in Britain, J. P. Donleavy or Thomas Pynchon in America) have relied upon their sense of the farcical and attempted a revival of the picaresque. Romain Gary, in France, had also wished after World War II to rally his contemporaries to a boisterous, would-be Rabelaisian novel and bluntly prophesied that "the novel of the future would be picaresque or it would not be." Little had those authors, or John Barth himself, reckoned with the inevitable monotony of the comic novel when it is not sustained by some intensity of feeling, some compassion, or some Chekhovian humor. After the first entertaining fifty pages, their puppets pall upon the reader. The drinking bouts of Pynchon's sailors in *V* and the mechanical sex orgies of others become invariably gloomy. Donald Barthelme, in *Snow White, City Life,* and in his recent collection of short stories, *Sadness,* fascinated and perhaps spoilt by the models of Kafka and Borges that have waylaid many an antinovelist lately, has attempted fractured tales and sophisticated stories in which irony and a sense of irrelevance constantly mock the reader who might be naive enough to look for a semblance of reality. From the start, the author lavishes clever hints to the effect that he would be the last person to give any credence to his own inventions. Kurt Vonnegut has likewise amused and entranced young readers through his affectation of anti-intellectual insolence and mild satire of our conventions. Our age has witnessed enough absurd crimes committed in the name of patriotism and of rationality to relish the satirical fiction of a new Swift or a new Voltaire. But it would require more powerful minds than Vonnegut's or Heller's to explode the pompousness of militarism, the conventions of logic, or the complacency of bourgeois society. The spiritual emptiness and the stylistic mannerism of *Cat's Cradle* and of *Welcome to the Monkey House* are lamentable. The critics, presumably mature, who have lavished praise upon Vonnegut seem to have been overeager to join the teenagers of 1970 in their boyish taste for the accumulation of absurdities.

Fantasy, if practiced with skill, has its place in literature and can serve as a healthy antidote for the high seriousness of the political pontiffs and the pharisees of our age. Yet Matthew Arnold's view of literature as likely to replace religion in our time cannot be dismissed so easily as mere Victorian cant. We have turned into a trite cliché the quip of Gide that bad literature is made out of good and well-meant feelings and intentions. Literature does not have to preach, or to distort truth, by representing good triumphing over evil. No ground, however perilous, is forbidden its practitioners. No one would contest its right to explore the rich themes of sex, crime, racial antagonism, violence, and madness. Nietzsche's motto could well be that of fiction writers in our time: "Dare ye be tragic, and ye shall be redeemed." In tragedy however, even at its most stark, in *Medea* or in *King Lear,* a spiritual purpose dawned somewhere, a moral direction could be dimly sensed by the watcher of *Oedipus Rex* or of *Phèdre.* Such was also the case for the great tragic novels, from Balzac to Hardy and Galdos. If today's readers feel alienated from the drama and fiction offered them, that is due to their inability to identify with any of the puppets whose wires are pulled by the authors of these fantasy-fictions. Many readers have become convinced that their lives are mechanized and meaningless, that they cannot thread their way among the inner conflicts which crucify them. Their solitude is pathetic; their neuroses haunt them; they have become convinced of their inability to prove adequate in sex, in love, in their home as parents, in the world at large as citizens. They would like to turn to literature so as to identify with characters who would illuminate their mazes of doubts and anguish. Young men who could not recognize their mothers or their female friends in *Generation of Vipers* or in Tennessee Williams' rabid females voice their disappointment at not finding one heroine, in the whole range of American fiction, with whom they could imaginatively or vicariously fall in love. Mothers, in the books they occasionally open, are all possessive furies. Women go about parties with cocktail glasses in their hands, howling for sex. Wives play a game of musical chairs with varied partners in suburbia, or they sneer scornfully at their mediocre husbands, as Janice does at pitiful, childish Harry Angstrom in Updike's *Rabbit* novels. Yet great themes for fiction are hardly lacking in our civilization, which is desperately fumbling for a new morality, yearning for a refuge from soul-harrowing work at the factory or at the office. The old and the middle-aged, just as much as the young, grope for some understanding of love, now that all prohibitions have been lifted; they seek it in vain in recent novels where, as an English reviewer put it, they are presented with nothing but tiresome orgies of "uninterrupted coitus."

Not fear of tragedy alone, but fear of beauty and fear of thought paralyze too many American writers. And the French, reacting against the existentialist literature of 1940-60 that had perhaps granted too much to philosophical speculation and to a search for ethical values under the guise of fiction, have become just as panicky, lest they might let any anthropomorphism creep into their fiction. Any return to the poetical prose of certain nineteenth-century novelists, or of Proust and Mann, would be unthinkable today; even Flaubert's slaving and moaning over his sentences strikes us as pathetically ludicrous. But in countries where literally millions of college graduates have received some training in English composition, it might be reasonable to hope for more enjoyment of aesthetic values than is provided by our bulky novels, suffering from a dreary poverty of vocabulary and from a simplified syntax. It may well be some day accounted a sad misfortune for American writing that so many of the cleverest writers of prose were first launched as contributors to *The New Yorker*. They cultivated a self-conscious, arch, and brittle style that may suit an occasional short story, but which soon becomes artificial when twenty such short stories are collected into a volume or when a grossly overpraised technician like Nabokov extends his display of virtuosity to the several hundred pages of *Ada*. Simplicity and naturalness are gifts that we all appear determined to wreck, if indeed we ever possessed them.

In the place of mature values and of characters who feel and think as adults, American fiction has concentrated its attention on the delineation of adolescents. *Tom Sawyer* and *Huckleberry Finn* were once banished from the children's department in many a public library in the United States. Fate has since taken its revenge. Those two books (the second of which is far superior to the first) have become the models for countless stories of teenagers engaged in roguish adventures and even more in a form of emotional masturbation. William Faulkner's Benjy has enjoyed a rich literary progeny, with the number of half morons who populate the tales of Salinger, Purdy, Vonnegut, and even Malamud's *Idiots First*. The influence of Hemingway on the writers whose vocation dawned in the 1950's may have wrought lasting harm to short story and fantasy-fiction writing. Norman Mailer, who, for all his failings, has occasionally dared to treat big themes, wryly remarked in his blatant *Advertisements for Myself* (1959):

> For all his [Hemingway's] size and what we have learned from him about the real importance of physical courage, he has still pretended to be ignorant of the notion that it is not enough to feel like a man: one must try to think like a man, as well.

In the same breath, Mailer derided Salinger, the creator of Holden Caulfield, the idol of many boys some fifteen years ago, as "the greatest mind ever to stay in prep school." A generation brought up on such narcissistic contemplation of itself not unsurprisingly failed sadly, in 1968-70, when, having frightened its elders with threats of revolution, it found itself incapable of devising anything constructive to put in the place of what it hoped to destroy. The issues in a modern world are economic and social and, fundamentally, more ideological than economic, and spiritual and religious. They could be brought home to us urgently by literature. Two or three novels of quality about the Vietnam war, dramatizing not only the hideousness of the senseless slaughter of civilian populations, but also the crises of conscience among officers, the loneliness and the sufferings of the soldiers, might have left a greater impact on American sensibility than all the reporting by journalists. So would fiction on the

Palestinians and the Israelis, on the poor and the unemployed in the United States, on the intellectuals and the ruling classes watching the collapse of a number of American myths and ideals. Neither the Germans nor the French have yet exorcized the ghosts of their shame at the sway of the Nazis over the near unanimity of the Germans, at the collapse of the ruling classes in France in 1940 and the sorrow and the pity of those who then gave up all hope for the recovery of freedom in their country. A few significant works of fiction, intensifying and individualizing their torn consciences, voicing their hopes, might have helped war-torn countries (now striving hard to forget their responsibilities and only half succeeding) cure themselves of what is corroding them. As "Rightly to be great/Is not to stir without great argument," in the words of Hamlet that De Gaulle was fond of quoting, great arguments and worthy themes for literature have not been lacking in our midcentury. Instead, Robbe-Grillet, one of the most skilled craftsmen of the recent French novel, peremptorily declared: "The writer is a man who has nothing to say. . . . To fancy that the novelist has something to say is the grossest of misconstructions." Le Clézio, one of the most promising of the very young novelists in France, after two or three near masterpieces, has since poured out a deluge of enumerations and of word collages, as if he had one concern uppermost in his mind: at any cost, to avoid writing anything that might look like a novel. Seldom has the hatred for literature appeared so blatantly among the very men who practice it and who live by it. And the scene for such a display of illwill is that same Paris where, not quite a hundred years ago, Mallarmé had assigned to poetry the noble mission of being nothing less than "the Orphic explanation of the earth."

No doubt, the authors themselves are to blame in the first place. Purposely and perversely, they enjoy keeping their readers at a distance, waylaying them in their labyrinthine paths, preventing them from experiencing sympathy, love or admiration, scorn or hatred for their characters. They choose instead to engage in private fights with language as the root of all deceptions and the tool of bourgeois privilege. Or else, they adopt a tone of cynical banter at all that is felt or thought by less sophisticated people than themselves. If they come to the English language from a foreign land, like Nabokov or Jerzy Kosinski, they like to display their recently acquired virtuosity through verbal inventiveness and exercises in self-conscious, mocking style. It is all very brilliant and very vain. Let the reader who might still yearn for social criticism, for delineation of manners, interpretation of life, or mere compassion and ordinary humanity turn elsewhere. This modern literature is not for him.

The critics were at first awed by the subtlety and the arrogance of these practitioners of fiction. Then they decided to prove even more clever and arrogant than the authors themselves. Imaginative literature serves them as a mere pretext for erecting around it a complex scaffolding of abstruse hermeneutics and of symbol deciphering. They have ransacked the arsenals of Freud, Rank, Jung, Reich, then those of the anthropologists and the linguists, in order to pin labels on fictional characters—where characters may still appear to have some reality. They have taught their students to look for the hidden structure or the esoteric symbols in the works they read. And, with a little ingeniousness, those indeed can be found. But they have not taught love for literature. Those same students, five years after they leave college, will read *The Wall Street Journal* (where the writing, at least, is of some quality), the sport pages and the comics in their newspaper, a few ephemeral works of documentary or biographical character (*Malcolm X, Blood in My Eye,* or *Soul on Ice*), occasionally a sexy story or one of those dreary volumes on "How to make your wife your mistress" or "How to cure psychic sexual impotence." Then one day, turning on their television, they hit upon *The Forsyte Saga* or *War and Peace,* and they are surprised to find out that literature, even transformed into another medium, can prove enjoyable and engrossing.

The most grievous fault, however, is the public's. We have been repeatedly deceived by reviews in which critics, for fear of not sensing the value of recent works and of repeating the gross mistakes of their predecessors, indiscriminately praise everything. We are being sent, by the several clubs of monthly or quarterly books, volumes that we do not enjoy. We are too sheepish to complain and revolt. Unable to sense anything human in the fictional characters of today, we believe ourselves to be nonhuman, or exceptional, or moronic, and we give up the attempt. Our authors have disregarded what long was the mythic function of literature—its struggle against what Malraux calls "the fatalities" threatening to crush us, and its ambition to endow with meaning a life that otherwise might be absurd. If the critics are too cowardly to oppose fashions, if the authors insist upon their systematic belittling and reviling of all that is human, it is up to the public itself to clamor that it deserves a better treatment. How sadly remote we are in modern America from the great voice of Walt Whitman who, just over a hundred years ago, assigned to literature a splendid role in the life of his country:

> Literature in our day and for current purposes is not only more eligible than all the other arts put together: it has become the only general means of morally influencing the world. (*Democratic Vistas,* 1871)

"Is Literature Dead? or Dying?" was delivered as the Keniston Lecture at the University of Michigan in 1972 and was subsequently published in the *Michigan Quarterly Review,* 12, No. 4 (Fall 1973).

# Index
# of Proper Names

DATE DUE